Human Factors in FORMS DESIGN

Human Factors in FORMS DESIGN

John H. Burgess

NELSON-HALL nh CHICAGO

LIBRARY OF CONGRESS CATALOGING IN PUBLICATION DATA

Burgess, John H.
Human factors in forms design.

Bibliography: p.
Includes index.
1. Business—Forms, blanks, etc. I. Title
HF5371.B84 1983 651'.29 83-6274
ISBN 0-88229-539-X

Manufactured in the United States of America

10 9 8 7 6 5 4 3 2 1

The paper in this book is pH neutral (acid-free).

CONTENTS

Preface vii

1. A Systems Approach to Forms Design 1

2. Information Requirements Analysis—A First Step 9

3. Human Engineering of Verbal Content 21

4. Human-Factors Principles Applied to the Form Configuration and Layout 27

5. Designing Forms Fill-In Instructions 47

6. An Evaluation of Some Common Government Forms 65

7. An Evaluation of Business-Form Applications and Design 109

8. The Design of Engineering Information-Gathering Forms 139

9. Processing and Using Forms-Derived Information 151

Appendix A
Sample Questionnaire Items 163

Appendix B
An Evaluation Checklist for Forms-Design Critique 167

Glossary 173
Bibliography 179
Index 187

PREFACE

For most of us, filling out a form can be an irritating and enigmatic experience. Instructions and layout may be difficult to follow. Color may be used inappropriately. Fill-in spaces may be crowded and required responses unclear. Perhaps worst of all, the form itself, or the information it generates, may seem inconsequential. We may even wonder whether the originators could not have done without it altogether.

At the national level, excessive forms and paperwork are responsible for a staggering waste of money, time, and manpower. Columnist Jack Anderson estimates that the cost to businesses and individuals comes to over $100 billion a year just to keep up with federal form requirements. Literally tons of government forms and questionnaires repose unread in federal files and warehouses. U.S. Senator John Glenn calls excessive paperwork the biggest hidden tax in America.

Within business organizations as well forms are often used inefficiently and unproductively. Indiscriminate distribution and bad design may needlessly impose complex demands on clients and reduce the overall productivity of employees.

After working in industrial and governmental bureaucratic settings for fifteen years and confronting the maze of forms from within and without, I became convinced that careful evaluation of, and improvements in, the forms-design process could save literally millions of dollars. Moreover, I felt that my human-factors background and perspective on the forms problem had equipped me to undertake the project. Human-engineering design approaches have proven highly successful in aerospace and industrial systems, and the application of these methods to forms design seemed long overdue.

Up to now, effective forms design has been addressed only tangentially in the human-factors and business literature. Human-factors literature is replete with material on lighting, character and color readability, and the like, while business literature deals exclusively with the flow and regulation of forms within the organization. But little attention is paid in either field to the efficiency and readability of forms or their cost effectiveness in use.

This text provides criteria for assessing the appropriateness of a form for a specific application and the efficiency of its design from a human-factors point of view. Its purpose is to help government and business administrators reduce costs and improve productivity.

Often government forms used for regulating, licensing, or tax assessment seem to victimize businesses or private citizens. Government agencies seem to be neither sensitive nor concerned with how difficult a form is to complete. Nor do they seem necessarily interested in alleviating the workload imposed on constituents. Government operations, however, are geared to efficiency and the prevention of error and possible loss of data. The Government Services Administration, for example, conducts comprehensive two-week courses on forms analysis and design to improve the efficiency of content and layout in capturing data.

The private sector's efforts to improve forms design concentrates on cost-effectiveness demonstrations showing where the profit margin is adversely affected by the use of poorly designed forms.

I also employ a broad systems view to relate the forms-design problem to total organizational goals. This perspective permits the reader to gain a pragmatic orientation when assessing faulty forms design. Evaluation criteria can then be meaningfully derived and related to required accuracy of data obtained from forms, such as cost to the organization, impact on profits, and other organizational measures. Forms evaluation exercises are included to give the reader a feeling for form quality.

This study is aimed principally at business and government administrators who wish to improve their forms-design programs. However, anyone concerned with improving the design or use of forms will find the material useful. Industrial engineering and business class instructors may also employ the evaluation techniques and design principles to advantage for instruction in forms design.

CHAPTER 1
A Systems Approach to Forms Design

Many forms used in government and business are incredibly complicated. As private citizens, we are all caught up in the complexity of forms use when we are required to file our income taxes, register our cars, or apply for a driver's license. Within business and government bureaucracies, the use of forms to obtain information consumes millions of hours annually.

Apart from the inordinate amount of time spent in filling out forms, the operation of society and the economy may be adversely affected by bad forms design. A medical doctor once commented that although he was interested in starting a Keogh plan, he gave up in dismay when confronted with the inordinately complex forms. A federal or state income tax form can frustrate and perplex even the college-educated respondent, who may find it difficult or impossible to understand why line 5 should be deducted from (or added to) line 15.

Often a form, or many of its items, may be unnecessary, or some other means of obtaining the necessary information may be preferable. A systems approach can be used to determine if a form is truly the best alternative for gathering necessary information. Then, human-factors analyses can proceed, incorporating principles of design that will save time and reduce error in filling out and processing the form.

TRADITIONAL FORMS DESIGN

The classical discipline of forms development is referred to as forms design. It consists of arranging data in their most useful form for transmission to those who require them, while eliminating redundancy and assuring economy in reproduction, procurement, handling, and filing.[1]

Forms design traditionally involves:

1. A form request and information specification from the originating office.
2. Design and layout.
3. Printing (including costing, procurement, and payment).
4. Forms storage and inventory control.
5. Forms distribution to, and completion by, the respondent.
6. Transmission of completed forms (duplicating, folding, addressing, mailing, and any other steps required to return the forms for processing).
7. Forms processing (data entry, computer programming, and massaging of data).
8. Data summary and presentation.

A SYSTEMS APPROACH

The sequences described above represent a typical development approach to forms design. This traditional approach generally involves a minimum of evaluation in the design process. A systems approach, on the other hand, includes an

1. N. L. Senensieb, "Corporate Systems and Procedures Responsibility" in *The Information Systems Handbook* edited by F. McFarlan and R. Nolan. Homewood, Ill.: Irwin, 1975, pp. 122-23.

analysis of forms effectiveness. This analysis projects and amplifies sufficient sequential details to make sound administrative judgments concerning the use of forms, while assessing other alternatives for collection of the data.

Method

The systems approach originated in aerospace and weapons development programs during the fifties. The analytical methods were developed to control the exceedingly complex nature of modern weapons and space systems, and were later adapted to domestic and industrial systems (Chapanis, 1970; McCormick, 1970; DeGreene, 1973). The approach has been described as looking at the forest as well as the trees to gain a total situational perspective (Melby et al., 1979).

Basically, a systems approach is the deliberate planning of a complex set of activities to accomplish specified purposes. The analytical procedure reduces a total complex system to subsets of activities which can be dealt with in analytical detail. By treating each detail as a component of the total interactive sequence, it is possible to evaluate its role in accomplishing total system goals.

Analytical developments in a systems approach to forms design include:

1. Defining system objectives (e.g., obtaining quantitative diagnostic information on the caseload of a general hospital in order to update space, equipment, and staff allotments).
2. Specifying the proposed information system (e.g., maintaining a data bank on patient diagnoses).
3. Listing functions necessary to obtain the information (e.g., reporting diagnostic information, converting it to machine-processable form, entering and processing data, and retrieving it for decision making).
4. Allocating functions (e.g., physicians report diagnoses, keypunch operators transfer data to computer cards,

operator enters the data, computer processes, stores, and retrieves it in summary form).

5. Analyzing the activities and tasks necessary for completion of the forms used in gathering diagnostic information.
6. Determining personnel or respondent population who will complete the forms (e.g., physicians).
7. Assessing skills required to complete the forms and determining the training or instructional aid required.
8. Evaluating the use of a form as compared with other means of obtaining the data. Evaluation consists of comparisons and trade-offs using costs against multiple criteria such as reliability and accuracy (e.g., would it be more efficient to phone the physician for the information, or would it be more efficient for the physician to interface with a computer terminal for data input?)

The systems approach to forms design is thus a projection of all sequences in forms processing, and an analysis of these to determine the advantage, if any, in the use of forms. During the analysis, characteristics of the respondent population are considered, and alternatives to the form are weighed. For example, a study of handwritten orders prepared by forty-seven physicians in a five-hundred-bed hospital showed that 16 percent had illegible handwriting, with another 17 percent barely legible. This resulted in a real loss in the effective working time of nurses and secretaries. Such a finding indicates the need for an alternative to the handwriting method of data input as far as physicians are concerned (Wright and Fraser, 1975), and the use of a form designed to eliminate handwritten responses would be recommended.

THE FORMS-DESIGN PROCESS

Once the decision has been made to use a form for data gathering, the forms-design process can begin. Figure 1.1

FIGURE 1.1
Functional flow chart of the forms-design process.

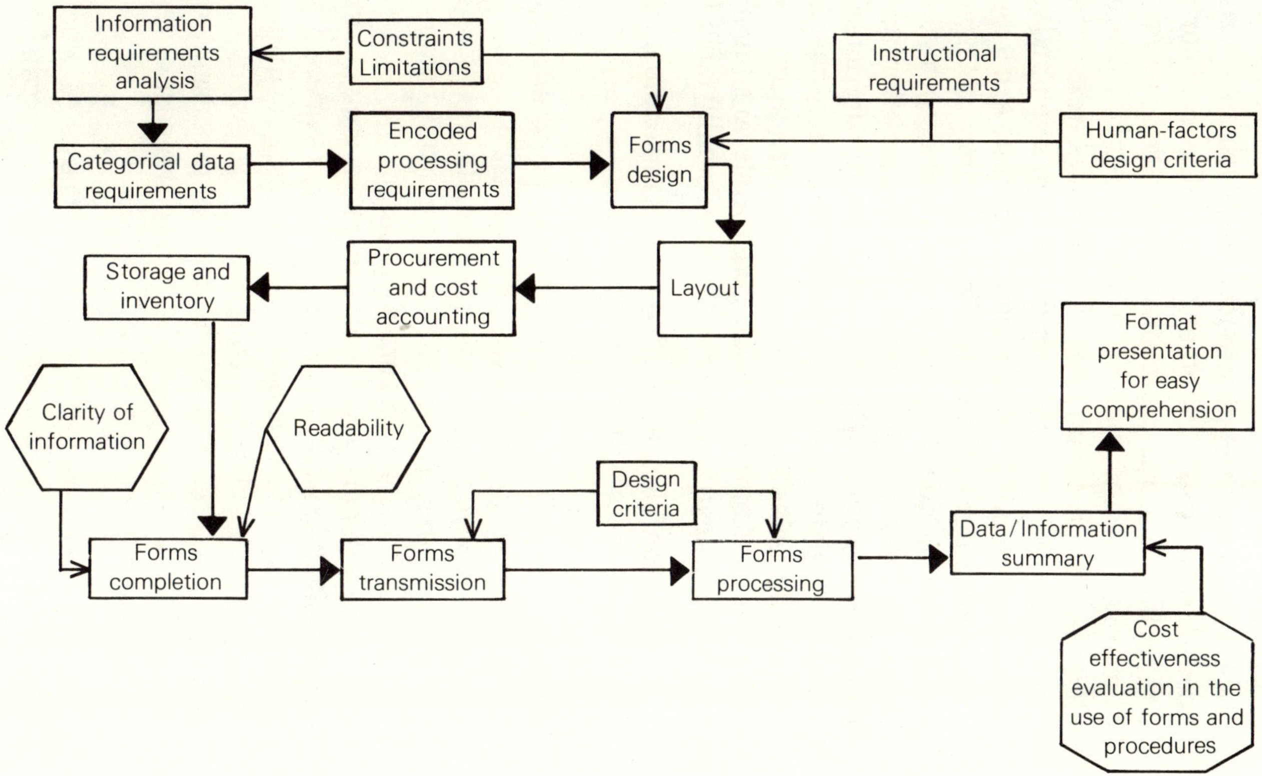

illustrates a sequential flow of development functions within the system. First, an "information requirements" analysis is needed to determine whether quantitative or discrete data are required for a decision, that is, numerical or yes-no type of information. Information categories and details to be included on the form can then be specified. Design criteria for the format are derived from the transmission-and-processing phase, which specifies whether the data are to be encoded for computers or manually worked up.

Constraints and limitations should be determined in advance in order to allow for their incorporation into forms design. For example, if the physicians entering diagnostic information prefer to write it out rather than check appropriate categories on the form, adequate space should be provided for this purpose. Such constraints are important in any forms-design program and may typically include:

1. Lack of confidence on the part of management in the form or in the information derived from it.
2. Excessively high printing costs.
3. Likelihood of clerical errors, errors in columnar entries, or marking-space errors.
4. High turnover of clerical personnel, necessitating frequent expensive retraining in the use of a complex form.
5. Inadequate filing and storage space.
6. Need for security for both raw and completed forms.
7. Inability to predict the number of copies needed, so extra copies might have to be made up quickly or surplus copies might have to be destroyed.
8. High cost of executive and clerical processing of forms (usually at least twenty-five times the cost of the forms themselves).

Instructional materials may be necessary when forms content is complex or equivocal. Instructions can be carried on the form itself or on adjunctive material.

During forms design, human-factors criteria must be incorporated into the format, content, and layout. Criteria can be developed after a study of the fill-in tasks, skills, and information levels of the respondent population and the kinds of environments in which the forms will be completed (e.g., desk, counter, truck cab).

After the design is completed, the procurement and cost accounting offices coordinate the form for production. The cost accounting department approves the funding, while the procurement department goes over the forms content and layout with the printer to assure accuracy. Final checking of form proofs from the printer must determine that the printed copies will be reproduced precisely as designed.

The printed forms are then stored and inventoried. Both blank and completed forms may require security measures to prevent access by unauthorized persons.

The forms completion process includes distributing the forms or making them readily available to the respondents at the required time. Reading and filling in the form should be accomplished efficiently and in the minimum possible time.

Transmitting and processing the completed forms must be considered in the design stage to allow for a number of possible uses: (1) decision making concerning individual cases, such as in employment applications or loan grants; (2) compiling in data banks, either in manual storage files or disc/ tape computer storage, and retrieving for auditing individual files and for statistical analysis; or (3) decision making concerning grouped data, such as those involving overall staffing requirements, the adequacy of building spaces, etc. The processing modes to be used will provide the criteria for designing the format of the form for manual or machine processing. For example, if automatic data-processing equipment is to be used, the responses must permit easy translation to keypunch cards or magnetic-reading equipment.

In the final phase of forms design, an important consideration is the manner in which the data will be submitted to the decision maker. When the completed forms themselves are used, as in applicant selection, the form should be easy and efficient for the respondent to complete and for the decision maker to interpret. Data summaries derived from the form, however, may require a special format. For example, computer printouts or terminal readouts should be provided free of programming artifacts to deliver succinct summary data precisely as determined in the information requirements analysis.

In assessing the use of the form for data gathering, cost effectiveness studies must involve both processing costs and operational criteria. Costing of the forms processing must include both expenses associated with the form itself, its engineering and procurement, and the total time and manpower costs involved in filling it out, processing it, and summarizing the data. In these studies, the operational criteria which can be used as performance measures include fill-in errors, uncompleted items or data losses, processing speed, accessibility and timeliness of the data, and its information value to the organization.

SUMMARY

A systems approach can provide a framework for cost-effectiveness evaluation in forms design. Early projection and assessment in the use of a form for specific data-gathering functions can assist the decision maker in determining if a form is the best alternative for the application in question. If it proves to be, then the forms-design process should begin with an information-requirements analysis. Formatting should be based on human-factors design criteria and manual or machine-processing requirements. The design process should further consider costs and uses to be made of the form, including the integration of data and their information value to the organization.

CHAPTER 2
Information Requirements Analysis—A First Step

The seemingly endless proliferation of forms in modern government and business environments may be due in part to a less-than-careful regard for how derived information is to be used. The accelerated electronic-data processing technology of the past two decades is also responsible for the so-called information explosion, which seems to have blown up as much into irrelevancy as relevancy (McKendry and Enderwich, 1967). While redundant data may often be preferred by decision makers, excessive information is of little value to the organization (Levine, 1973).

Characteristic input on forms for electronic data processing often seems to be a kind of random selection of data items without regard to the questions they are meant to answer. Important information considerations are neglected: "Why do you want these data? How will you use them? What will they tell you, and for what purpose?"

Information to be derived from a form may require that either precise quantitative measures be filled in or a more simple listing of categories be checked off. Form entries which require a precise digital input, such as weight or age, could, in some cases, be reduced to checking off a categorical range of values, for example, "20 to 25," "26 to 30," and so on. Where these categorical information items will serve the purpose of the decision maker, they should be preferred in the interest of simplification.

Using an information-requirement approach also necessitates that a rationale be provided to justify the inclusion of each item: "How will you use demographic information?" "When you query about socioeconomic status, why do you need income information when you have educational level?" And so on.

Such clarification of the overall requirement for a form and the need for each item can help prevent the excessive use of forms and enhance form quality early in the development process.

AN INFORMATION-ANALYSIS PROCEDURE

In forms design, the initial step following a forms request must involve assurance of information value. A forms request or order describes the purpose, identifies the persons or respondents from whom the information is to be obtained, and specifies to whom the information is to go and why it is wanted. Also included are required form quantities, duration of expected use, and how information is to be processed. This provides the forms-control group with a background orientation on which to base the information analysis. A careful information-requirements analysis is undertaken to assure that only necessary information will be included on the form. The analysis may begin with interviews of the persons requesting the form, followed by rational analyses to establish value and validity of each information item to be included on the form.

The information analysis involves the following:

1. Establishing definite information goals to be accomplished by those requesting the form (e.g., a company might want to identify the source and frequency of customer complaints in order to undertake remedial action).
2. Assuring that a form is the best way to obtain the information (e.g., personal contact in the field would entail excessive travel expense).
3. Describing the form to be used and identifying areas of information to be obtained (e.g., a customer-complaint form might be employed to provide information on sources, nature, and frequency of customer complaints).
4. Providing a rationale for each information item (e.g., a source item might be included to trace the cause of the complaint).
5. Determining what actions can be based upon information derived from the form (e.g., changes in manufacturing, packaging, customer relations, etc.).
6. Deleting items on which action cannot be taken (e.g., if it is not feasible to change manufacturing, then that item should be omitted).

The process is iterative or developmental, as illustrated in the feedback loops of figure 2.1.

Goal Definitions

The forms-control group, as illustrated in figure 2.2, may undertake the analysis beginning with the form order. First, the initiating group should be contacted to clarify its requirements. For example, if the initiating group is in a sales-management operation, it may need information concerning customer relations. The forms-control group would ask the nature of the customer relations to be probed and the

FIGURE 2.1
A forms-information development process.

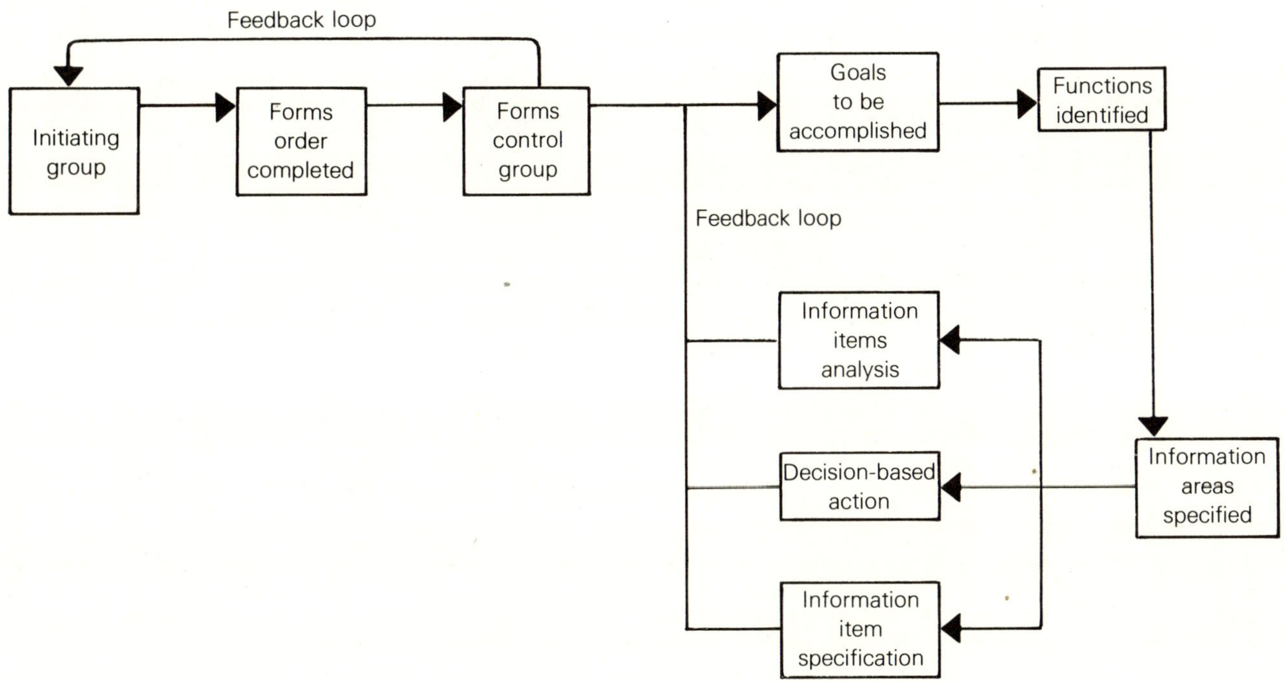

information purposes for which the form is to be used. Information questions to be put to sales management might include:

1. What is the precise nature of the problem?
2. How is it evidenced by actual hard data?
3. What functional areas are involved in the problem?
4. What would the management solutions be to the problem?
5. Why was a form chosen as the device for obtaining the information?

Upon completing the interview, it might be found that the problem was identified by an excessive number of customer complaints. The sales supervisors, faced with such a problem, might decide a questionnaire method would best determine why the customers were complaining, and that a forms approach would be most economical, since their salespeople and customers were widely scattered and the mailed form would obviate excessive travel by the management staff.

On the other hand, if in turning to hard data on rates of customer complaints registered, the forms-control group finds that these were not excessive, administrators may be dissuaded from using a form. Instead, a small number of customers and salespeople might be sampled to resolve the problem. However, if a rate of, say, ten complaints per one hundred customers per month is found and is considered to have a critical effect on sales relations, then a forms approach for a broad coverage could be more pertinent.

The management response to customer complaints thus might be to develop a permanent information-collecting system that would serve to pinpoint critical areas and provide a basis for continual monitoring of customer relations. The sales-management goals should be quantified in order to provide a basis for assessment of program effectiveness. (For example, the goals might be to reduce the number of customer complaints by 50 percent within a six-month period, and to keep the complaint level below five per one hundred customers per month.)

IDENTIFYING PERTINENT FUNCTIONS

Functional areas involved in customer complaints must be determined in order to establish content for the customer-complaint form. Figure 2.2 presents a general flow of functions which involve possible areas concerned in the customer-complaint analysis.

1. Sales representative customer contacts
   a. frequency and timeliness of contacts
   b. accessibility to customer
   c. adequacy of information to the customer
2. Order placement
   a. timeliness
   b. convenience
   c. accuracy
3. Delivery promise
   a. timeliness and reasonableness
   b. accuracy
   c. honesty and reliability
4. Production scheduled and/or inventory draw
   a. priority
   b. slippage
   c. progress reporting to customer
5. Packing
   a. damage to merchandise due to packaging and/or lack of protection
   b. reliability in inclusion of parts
6. Storage
   a. environmental and handling damage
7. Invoicing
   a. accuracy of listing
   b. reliability of parts packing

FIGURE 2.2
Functions and sequences involved in customer complaints.

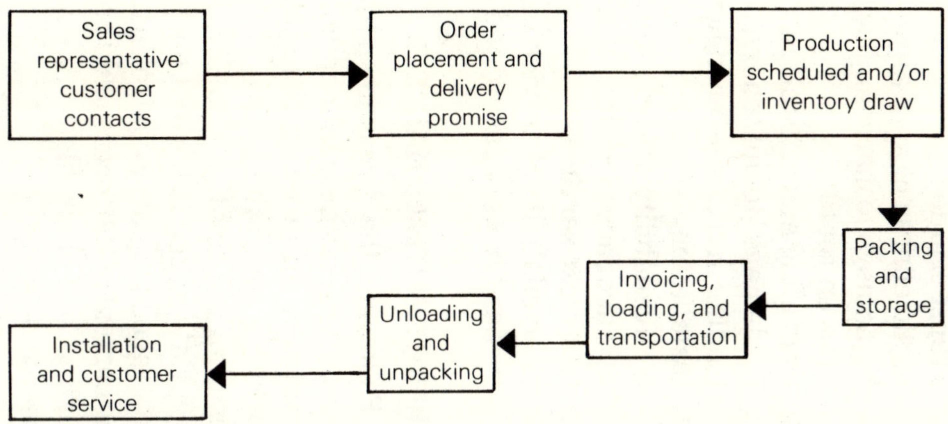

8. Loading
    a. timeliness of shipping
    b. damage to merchandise due to handling for on-loading and load seating
9. Transportation
    a. timeliness of arrival
    b. damage to merchandise due to impact and accelerations en route
10. Unloading and unpacking
    a. damage to merchandise due to handling in off-loading and customer in-house handling
11. Installation
    a. availability of service engineers
    b. adequacy of installation service
12. Customer services
    a. availability of service engineers
    b. timeliness of repair and maintenance service

INFORMATION ITEM ANALYSIS

Following the breakdown of product-processing functions, required general content areas of the form can be developed. In order to determine what might be causing customer complaints, each area must be investigated. The resulting information would enable management to take appropriate action to correct the problem(s). If the complaints are traced to quality control in manufacturing, for example, the content of the form should be structured to illuminate the quality-control problem. A quality-control solution could then be developed.

Based on the functional areas of concern listed above, the following items might be included on the form.

1. Customer's name, department, and spokesperson
2. Product about which complaint was registered
3. Salesperson and date of sale

4. General area of complaint
   a. placing order
   b. delivery
   c. quality of merchandise
   d. condition of merchandise
   e. installation, repair, and/or maintenance
5. Action to be taken
   a. sales procedure correction
   b. production improvement
   c. storage improvement
   d. shipping procedure improvement
   e. transportation improvement
   f. service and installation improvement

INFORMATION-ITEM SPECIFICATION

Initially, the form is best structured with an open-ended format to obtain detailed information from which specific items can be derived. A preliminary form addressing customer complaints should ask general questions, inquiring about major areas of complaints, such as merchandise quality, transportation problems, service improvements, or damaged goods. From initial responses in such a pilot study, the specific content areas can be more accurately specified, and forms design can begin.

INFORMATION ISSUES WITHIN AN ORGANIZATION

Information to be included in the development of a form—whether an employment application blank, an invoice, or a complaint information form—must relate to the purposes for which the information is being sought. Broad organizational goals often prove too general as a basis for justifying specific form developments (Stamper, 1975). For that reason, information requirements ideally originate with those departmental groups who are attempting to accomplish specific purposes that are tied to broader organizational goals (Lurie, 1962; Berger, 1971).

Technical information on operational problem areas within an organization can almost always be obtained in the local work environment. The greater the volume of information available within the local environment, the more effective the solution that management might formulate (Hodges and Angalet, 1968; Levine et al., 1975).

In developing items to address to personnel either in or out of the local organization, repetitive items and remote contingency questions should be deleted (Mahoney, 1958). Items that are resourceful, to the point, and action oriented are best for direct-action decisions. Eliminating irrelevant items reduces costs in forms development, completion, and processing.

While the substantive nature of the forms project may largely determine the amount of information to be captured, careful trade-off studies are necessary to eliminate low-yield items. The questionnaire form on customer complaints, for example, may contain a great many demographic items, such as sex, age, occupation, and income. If any of these cannot be demonstrated to carry information important to alleviating complaints, they should not be included on the form.

When formulating questions for a business form, a hypothetical cost-versus-value-of-information break-off point might be established as illustrated in figure 2.3. In limiting the number and scope of questions to be included on the form at the outset, only those of greatest relevancy to the problem should remain. In the example given of customer complaints, valuable information that could be used to trace and correct sources of complaints could be obtained at considerably less cost if items of minimal information value were removed from the form. Including items that are only tangentially related to the solution of complaint problems would increase the form operating costs without

FIGURE 2.3
Hypothetical information-value trade-off, cost, and point of diminishing returns.

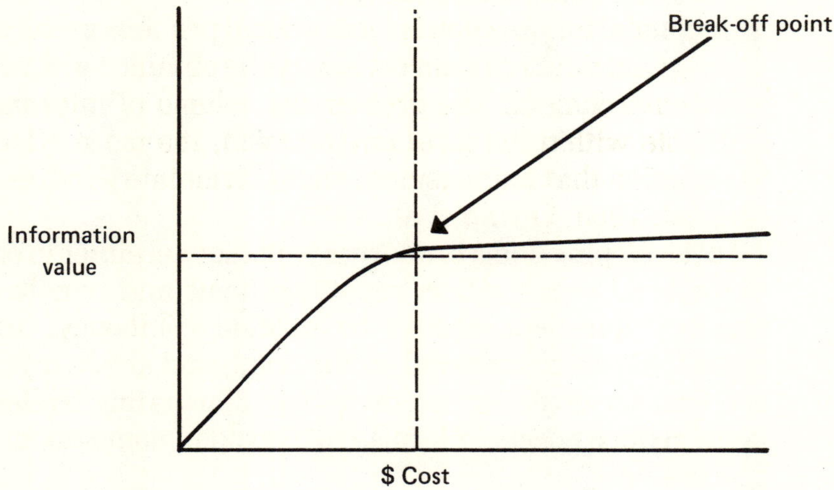

appreciably benefiting the analysis. Manpower and time required in obtaining the information, filling in the form items, and processing the data greatly increase the cost, but may be of little or indeterminate value in accomplishing sales-management goals.

Summary

Applying the information-requirement analysis procedure used in human engineering of matching systems to forms design can help reduce the number of unnecessary forms and improve the quality of information derived from them. How this can be done is illustrated by the development of a customer-complaint form to be used for identifying and alleviating the sources of complaints. Analytical caveats are described to prevent the inclusion of low-yield information items of a form, thus enhancing its value while decreasing its cost.

CHAPTER 3

Human Engineering of Verbal Content

An information analysis provides reasonable assurance that the use of a form is the best alternative for acquiring the data. The analysis also establishes the items that will have the greatest information value. The next step is to develop verbal content (words and sentences) for easy comprehension by the respondent.

Most forms designers have good verbal ability, but this alone does not guarantee that they will develop effective form content. Most importantly, they must be sensitive to the respondent population and understand how the verbal content can best be structured for reliability and accuracy of response.

In general, the verbal content should be terse, and the designer should use only words that are familiar to the respondent. Ambiguity should be avoided, as should compound questions and the unwarranted use of technical terms.

TERSENESS

A form should be uncluttered for easy reading, so avoid lengthy sentences or phrases. Where possible, use one-word items to elicit the response. For example, use "Name" rather than "What is your name?" When sentences are necessary, keep them short, in the active voice, and make positive statements.

Sentence Length

If sentences have more than one verb, suspect them of being too long. Nested clauses in a sentence may confuse a reader. Avoid phrases like "the customer who complained to the salesperson who sold the gears that were damaged" (Blumenthal, 1966). They only lead to confusion and error.

Active Voice

Studies also indicate that active-voice sentences are easier to understand and remember than passive-voice sentences. "Attach the invoice" is better than "The invoice should be attached."

Positive Statements

Sentences with negative words, such as *not, except, unless,* are more difficult to understand than affirmative statements (Jones, 1961; Anisfeld and Klenbort, 1973). Double negatives are even more confusing in a form: "Do not fill in this item if you have not contacted the salesperson" is harder to understand than "Complete this item if you have contacted the salesman."

Studies show that positive statements elicit more positive responses, even when their negative counterparts are easy to understand. "Leave this space blank" is preferable to "Do not write in this space." Items that ask the respondent to check what *does* apply are clearer than items that ask the respondent to check what *does not* apply. Words such as *reduce,* and negative prefixes such as *un-*, *dis-*, or *in-*, are also more difficult to understand than positive phrasing (Clark and Chase, 1972). The word *more* is easier to understand than the word *less* (Palermo, 1973). Example: "Complete this item if amount is more than..." rather than "...if the amount is less than...."

Familiarity

Authorities recommend the use of only familiar words in forms design. Familiar words are obviously easier to understand than less familiar words, yet forms designers frequently include uncommon words. Studies show that common words are easier to read and respond to than are less familiar words (Loftus et al., 1970: Wright and Barnard, 1975). This applies to abbreviations as well.

Even familiar terms may have different meanings, such as "total income," which could mean either before or after taxes. "Family" also might mean, for some, relatives next door who come over for meals. Even familiar words require empirical testing to assure that a common meaning operates.

Ambiguities

Words or statements that are ambiguous frequently result in poor item reliability and data loss. Moreover, the respondent may be unaware that the item is equivocal and respond without even questioning its meaning (Wright, 1969). For example, the item "Complaint received on," could refer to the date, but a respondent may fill in a description of the complaint as an obvious answer.

The inconsistent use of words may also result in ambiguity, for example, "Where both the supervisor and salesperson are in contact with the customer, management should complete the item." Such ambiguities can be controlled by using specific, complete, and consistent terms, such as, "date complaint received" and "supervisor should complete the item."

Compound Questions

Form items that combine two or more alternatives within one question may confuse a respondent. For example, "Was the sale made within New York State and under $10,000.00?" Respondents tend to answer one or the other question, but not both (Trabasso, 1971). Over one-third of typical respondents either leave these items blank or respond incorrectly. Disjunctions and conjunctions should be avoided when formulating forms content and single-element questions preferred.

Technical Terms

Terms included in a form are often familiar to forms designers and administrators but perplexing to a respondent. For example, the Internal Revenue Service Form 4562 on depreciation uses the "Accelerated Cost Recovery System." Even though explained in the instructions, the technical jargon confounds many respondents, for example, farmers who might lack the necessary accounting background for understanding. The complex use of adjectival modifiers has also been found to confuse the reader (Blumenthal, 1966).

Item Structure

Only limited study has been completed to date on how questions can best be formulated or formatted. Yet the way in which the content is presented to a respondent may be of major importance to comprehension (Brown, 1971). Alternative item structures, as illustrated here, for example, require evaluation for effectiveness in eliciting responses.

1. I make my customer contacts: – weekly – semimonthly – monthly – semiannually.

(Circle the one that applies)

2. Are your customer contacts made weekly? ____
semimonthly ____
monthly ____
semiannually ____
(Please check one of the above)

3. How often do you make customer contact?

A number of different question structures are presented in Appendix A. However, research has not yet established which styles are most effective for comprehension and in eliciting reliable responses (Osgood et al., 1957; Wright and Barnard, 1975).

Testing for Comprehension

In order to be reasonably assured that the forms content will be understood by the respondent population, a preliminary draft of the form should be prepared. A small sample of three to five might be employed, but respondents must be truly representative of the population, for example, middle-aged housewives or industrial-machine salespeople. More extensive oral interviews can be made using this sample, questioning the meaning of each item and how the respondent interprets the content.

Empirical testing of a larger sample (thirty or more respondents) might also be done with written interviews. Respondents might be asked to explain the meaning of terms used in the form. If the sample is large enough, the proportion of respondents giving correct interpretations should be approximately the same as could be expected in the general respondent population.

Content difficulties can be detected quickly in such pilot studies, even before the form design and layout begins.

SUMMARY

Forms content must be developed to assure that respondents will understand precisely what is being asked. Verbal content should be terse, in the active voice. Statements should be positive. Items must be consistent and have specific reference. Double negatives, compound meanings, and technical terms with which respondents might not be familiar should be avoided. Structure of the form questions is important, but the effectiveness of different styles of questions has yet to be determined. Pilot studies are required in forms development to assure that the content will be understood by the respondent population.

CHAPTER 4
Human-Factors Principles Applied to the Form Configuration and Layout

The design goal in form development is to come up with an easily understood form that produces complete, reliable and accurate information. Design objectives include the development of a form that impels the respondent to complete all the data spaces, that ensures consistent interpretations of words and symbols, and that elicits fill-in responses that are precise enough to meet the information requirements of the originator. Data must also be easily processed or readable on a file-by-file or summary basis. The design orientation in a governmental organization may be somewhat different from that of a business operation, but essential forms-design objectives must remain the same.

As stated in the preceding chapter, an effective verbal content must be established for the form, after which the arrangement of the content for easy reading and fill-in response must be assured. In this chapter, human-engineering principles that can be applied to problems of forms perception and execution are presented.

Human-factors principles and design practices that have proven effective in man-machine interactions can also be applied to the design of form configurations. Principles established for display-reading efficiency, quick recognition of display elements, and efficient manual execution of required machine input may be applied to the mechanics of forms operations.

THE FORM-COMPLETION TASK

A typical respondent's form-completion task includes the following elements:

1. Identifying and acquiring the form.
2. Scanning the form by information blocks to determine information needed.
3. Assembling information documents, reports, notes, and correspondence necessary to complete the form.
4. Reading each information and entry requirement to determine required response.
5. Finding or recalling appropriate information element.
6. Filling in form spaces with appropriate responses.
7. Signing or otherwise certifying information.
8. Returning or mailing form for processing.

In reviewing the respondent's task, operational design requirements can be derived to develop criteria for design solution. Form development requirements might therefore be described as follows:

1. Efficient forms circulation through:
   a. easy alphanumeric and sign recognition
2. Scanning ease through:
   a. easy readability
   b. forms-organization efficiency
   c. quick-recognition symbols and codes

3. Good forms reading speed and accuracy through:
   a. efficient content design
   b. easy readability
4. Efficient forms completion through:
   a. marking-task efficiency
   b. rapid completion time
5. Effective forms summarization and action through:
   a. efficient distribution control
   b. built-in processing provisions
   c. information feedback provisions to assure corrective action

The above design requirements may then be translated into categorical human-engineering design standards as follows:

1. Forms and component recognizability
   a. color, size, shape, and space coding
   b. signage (symbols)
2. Forms readability
   a. optimal printing design
   b. organization of sections and blocks
3. Forms input
   a. efficient layout for manual response

DESIGNING FOR FORMS RECOGNIZABILITY

Forms, sections of forms, and components within sections can be made more easily recognizable through the use of various coding techniques. Headings can be used effectively, as can the classical visual coding techniques of color, spatial, size, and shape differences. Pictorial elements may also be employed to advantage in forms design.

Headings

Efficiency in understanding a passage in prose has been found to be greatly enhanced by the use of headings and subheadings (Dooling and Lachman, 1971). Headings can be effectively designed using either words or coded symbols to identify the form, its contents, and/or its sections.

Coding

The use of codes in forms configurations can be effective if properly applied. In color codes, the colors used must be easy to discriminate from one another. The immediate interpretability of a code is also important if it is to have recognition value. Valuable form space might be wasted if shape or geometric codes are used in addition to word descriptions. Code-recognition values must be assessed against form design constraints and overall design effectiveness.

Color Coding

Color printing costs are more than those for black and white, particularly where multiple colors are used in the form design. However, when color coding is employed, improved reliability and accuracy could more than pay for extra printing expenses in time savings for those filling in the forms.

Careful selection must be made in the use of colors, since one male in twenty has color-defective vision. Yellow, blue, red, orange, purple, and buff are most generally distinguishable by a color-defective subject.[1]

Color coding of forms is most effective when agreed-upon standards of significance for specific colors are employed. For example, red might be used for critical areas, such as amounts owed or overdrawn, while yellow could call attention to circumstances, such as customer complaints and where discounts or other remedies must be applied. Research indicates that if color standards of significance are employed and understood, color can aid both in searching

1. Refer to color designations in Federal Specification TTC 595.

for areas of information to be isolated and in identifying their nature (Shontz et al., 1971; Christ, 1975).

Size Coding

Size coding might be employed in a number of ways in forms design, such as larger letters to highlight a category or item, square boxes to be filled in by females, round boxes by males, and the like. Such coding, however, must be logically developed and pretested to assure an effective response (Hammer and Ringel, 1965).

Shape Coding

Shape coding could take the form of various representations to facilitate quick recognition of items on a business or engineering form. For example, silhouettes of various recognizable appliances, people, or vehicles could signal an area of content or a section of a form. Multiple geometric shapes are also easily discriminated visually. These require prior identification, however, to be employed meaningfully in forms design. Any shape codes used should be pretested to assure consistent and reliable response.

Space and Group Coding

Form items are more easily read when grouped by area of inquiry and set off by appropriate spaces. Identifying information such as name, address, and marital status could comprise one group, for example, and work history and various places of employment another. Spatial coding is already used extensively in forms design, but its effectiveness could be improved.

Pictorial Symbols

Pictorial elements, along with various shapes and silhouettes, can be used to augment words. Smith (1981) found that pictures could be effectively used to clarify control-display relations, labels, and word usage. Male engineers and a general population of females were used as subjects to respond to various sketches pertaining to required control action and word usages. They were asked, for example, to indicate which way a control should move to regulate a display element. The use of pictures to illustrate relationships was found to be an effective mode of communication. Other studies also illustrate the value of well-designed pictorial symbols for identifying automobile dashboard controls (Green and Pew, 1978) and for directing motorists to required gas-line queues (Parsons, 1979).

FORMS READABILITY

Readability hinges not only on good verbal content, but also on the printing used, including color, contrast, style of lettering, and on paper texture. Appropriate sequencing, sectionalizing, and blocking out of the material of the form can also appreciably enhance comprehension.

Optimal Printing

The readability of print is a function of colors used, contrast effects, size and relatively proportioned height, stroke, and width of the print, and, finally, the style of the letters and numerals. The paper and its texture are also important to readability.

Print Color

Sharpness of letters, numerals, and words depends on contrast and color. The most vivid contrast is black on a white background. Readability is positively or negatively affected by the use of different colored backgrounds and colored markings. Red and orange stand out best against a blue-green background. Also, several combinations of color markings are best—red on white and bright green, black, or blue on a bright yellow background.

Print Contrast

Readability is best when light reflected from the print differs in intensity up to 100 percent from that of the background, as in the case of white on black.

$$\text{Percent contrast} = \frac{B_1 - B_2}{B_1}$$

where B_1 is the brightest of the two measures and B_2 is the lesser brightness

Color contrast of print is often neglected when electronic-data processing is employed. Light blue or pale green print are often used so that the electronic reader will not read certain parts of the form, such as instructions. It should be borne in mind, however, that respondents will also have difficulty reading these low-contrast colors (Poulton, 1969).

Print Dimensions and Character Style

Recommended character dimensions and style are illustrated in figure 4.1. Reading of lower-case letters is generally found easier than reading upper-case (Tinker, 1965; Poulton, 1968; Gray, 1975). However, upper-case print may be effectively employed in headings.

Print size should be a minimum of 8 point for easy reading. Eight point size print is roughly one-twelfth of an inch or around 2 millimeters in height. Seventy-two points equal one inch. Smith (1979) found that a visual angle subtended of 10 to 24 minutes of arc assured good readability. This is equivalent to 8 point size print at a 20 to 28 inch reading distance. Print size should be increased when the respondents are elderly or have diminished visual acuity.

Stroke and Width

The stroke-to-height ratio of the print should be about one to eight. Character width should be about 70 percent of the height for easy reading.

FIGURE 4.1
Recommended print dimensions and character style.

A B C D E F G H I J K L M
N O P Q R S T U V W X Y Z
0 1 2 3 4 5 6 7 8 9

Characters widely used in military applications (MIL Standard MS 33558, ASG, Air Force-Navy Drawing 10400)

Width should be approximately 70% of the height

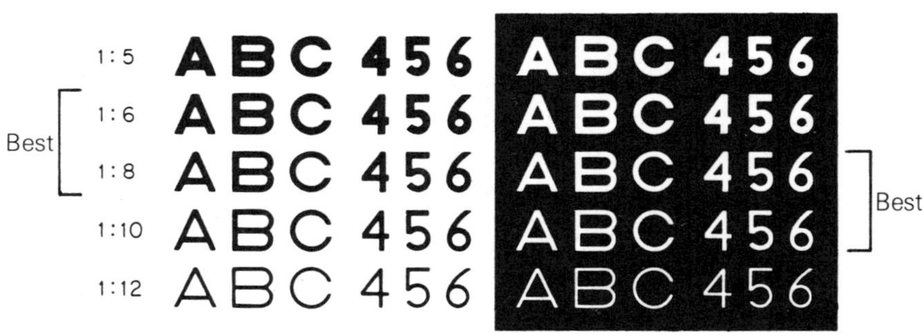

Ratio of stroke width to character height

Unembellished

Embellished

Character Style

Embellishments, flares, and segmentation of letters and numerals slow down recognition. Unembellished characters, as illustrated in figure 4.1, are more easily readable (Van Nes and Bouma, 1980).

Paper

Nonglossy paper that is thick enough to prevent see-through should be used.

Lighting

Readability of forms material presupposes adequate lighting. Reliable reading may be assured at levels above 25 Millilamberts of white-light illumination, which allows for adequate color perception. A Millilambert is approximately one Footcandle, i.e., white paper at one foot from a candle. Daylight illumination may vary from 100 to 10,000 Millilamberts. An illumination level of 100 Millilamberts provides for good visual acuity and all normal visual functions.

FORM ORGANIZATION

Readability is also enhanced by effective arrangement of forms material into logical sequences and perceptual groups.

Logical Sequencing

Logical sequencing facilitates easy comprehension. For example, a customer-complaint form may present the customer's name, business, and the nature of the complaint, in that order. Then, a general-to-specific sequence may follow with identification of the complaint area and associated circumstances, responsible production or service categories, and the specific corrective action required.

Sectionalizing

By seeing the various parts of the form grouped into general categories of information, the respondent can more easily grasp the content of the form. Sectionalizing can be especially useful when an extensive array of information is presented in blocks for easy perceptual breakdown by the respondent.

Temporal Sequencing

Research has demonstrated that when the order in which procedures are mentioned matches the order in which they are to be carried out, the instructions are much more readily understood (Clark and Clark, 1968). A confusing order, such as "Before filling out Section 2, read the instructions on page 2," could be more effectively sequenced to read: "Read the instructions on page 2. Then fill in Section 2."

Word Arrangement

Horizontal layout of letters and words, rather than vertical, generally provides for better readability.

This
arrangement
is more
difficult
to read

than the normal left-to-right arrangement, which is consistent with normal reading habits (Coleman and Hahn, 1960; Williams, 1966). For easy visual scanning, length of sentences or legends generally should not exceed fifteen to thirty picas, where six picas equal one inch.

Layout Plane

A number of typographical arrangements are possible for distinguishing headings among the form sections. Studies have shown, however, that any departure from a horizontal arrangement adversely affects readability. Headings printed sideways, even though they may bracket several rows of questions related to the same topics, are less effective than horizontal headings (Kolers, 1968).

Clutter and Separation

Readability is also affected by the density and arrangement of material within a form. Drury and Clement (1978) found that although the increased density of a visual field increases the scanning or search time, the time can be reduced by grouping the characters into visual patterns. The implication for forms design is that content should be minimized. Effective grouping to increase the separation and density of each group should also enhance readability.

Where pictorial or geometric symbols are used to augment word descriptions, these should be sufficiently separated from the word to prevent recognition interference (Noyes, 1980). In word recognition, the word is first located, and the beginning of the word is then identified. Surrounding distractors are ignored, and the word is read. When symbolic characters are similar in shape or size to the first letter of the word, the word-reading speed is slowed. The symbol therefore should be sufficiently separated from the word to prevent reading interference.

Configurational Arrangement

Organization of a form into easily perceived configurations can also improve readability. Sections of a form might be organized into quadrants for visual grouping of form components that must be completed. Quadrants or other similar arrangements can be more easily checked and there would be less likelihood of missing a section to be completed. Completed forms could be so configured that all marks to be filled in would be aligned or would form a pattern. Such configurations of fill-in marks would also facilitate the final check of a form to assure that all answers have been completed.

FORMS INPUT

Forms design should permit a respondent to complete the fill-in task conveniently and efficiently. Yet designers are often concerned with administrative tasks and neglect the needs of the respondent. For example, the respondent can follow a fill-in requirement more easily if the answer space is close to the question, but the forms-processing task is easier if the answers are all grouped together on one part of the page. The designer who neglects the respondent's preference and gives precedence to the forms-processing task may also inadvertently confound the administrative task, because it requires more administrative time to handle incomplete or improperly done forms. Empirical evaluation or predesign testing is the best way to arrive at a design compromise between the respondents and the forms-processing task.

All forms consist of a title, instructions, introduction, body (or material to be completed), and routing directions. In order to accommodate the respondent during forms design, it becomes necessary to assess the forms reading and input tasks associated with each layout, and, as much as possible, to simplify these.

Task Simplification

The respondent's task in completing a form consists of identifying the form and its sections, scanning the items to be filled in, and choosing the writing instrument to be used. Information might also have to be assembled where immediate recall will not suffice to complete an item. The method of marking must be decided or determined; then the item must be traced or tracked to its marking space.

Simplifying these tasks can be accomplished by deleting any unnecessary items, proper sequencing in the form layout, providing adequate space for entries, and providing fill-in aids. The required manual fill-in responses should be designed for consistent and reliable input in a minimum of time.

Sequencing

Proper sequencing in forms design should include:

1. Standard layout sequences (instructions at the top, routing at the bottom, and the like).
2. Consecutively numbered steps throughout, beginning with introductory and instruction sections and continuing through the body, closing, follow-up, and routing sections.

Space

The efficient use of space on forms entails:

1. Minimal margins to conserve paper.
2. Statements, rather than questions, to conserve reading time and space (e.g., "Name" is more economical than "What is your name?")
3. Sufficient space provided for the expected length of the entry.

Failure to allow sufficient space is one of the most common deficiencies in forms design. Space required to write names and street addresses, cities, zip codes, phone numbers, and, particularly, to complete the information needed for a narrative item is certainly a basic design consideration. Space requirements should be studied in predesign to assure that even elderly respondents will be able to fill in the information without crowding and hesitation.

Fill-in Aids

Where items involve signs or symbols, such as dollar and cent signs, decimal points, and semicolons, the respondent's task can be simplified by including these in the answer spaces. Computer-processed forms can also employ stored data to print out names and identification numbers to relieve a respondent of an additional fill-in task.

Manual Entry

When forms are poorly designed, respondents may find form-entry requirements confusing or they may have to study the form just to become familiar with how the entries are to be made. When the information required is too precise, the respondent may have to refer to files or to research material. This results in delays and data being left out. Manual fill-in time is prolonged if a form has instructions on the back or if items are visually obstructed by one's hand or a typewriter roller. The following forms-design principles are recommended to improve the forms-entry task:

1. Straightforward entry requirements should be stated. The form should not demand extensive preparation, integration, or prior processing of information to be completed.
2. Specific marks to be made or required entry responses should be clearly indicated.
3. Only consistent fill-in locations should be used, with entries made at the right side to preclude covering the item with the hand. Spotty, scattered fill-in spaces should be avoided.
4. Readouts or legends should be oriented at normal reading angles to avoid the need for turning the form (or the head) to read the material.
5. Fill-in instructions should be on the same side of the sheet as the entry they refer to. Turning the sheet over to obtain instruction is time consuming and can result in memory error.

6. Captions and legends should appear consistently in the upper left-hand corner, where they will not be obscured by the hand or typewriter roller.
7. A ballot-box type of entry format should be employed for single entries.
8. Blank lines should be used for narrative entries. Research has shown that space subdivisions, where one letter per space is required, reduce legibility and entry time. Vertical space marks designed for each letter are more disruptive than complete boxes (Barnard and Wright, 1975).
9. Fill-in blocks and spaces should be aligned close to the item for entry. Two- or three-inch gaps between the item and the entry box introduce error. Copying information across such gaps results in transcription errors, and the bigger the gap, the greater the error frequency (Conrad and Hull, 1967).

AN ILLUSTRATED FORMS DESIGN

Figure 4.2 illustrates a hypothetical form incorporating human-factors design principles. The content is based on the customer-complaint information requirements described in chapter 2.

The design includes features that enhance a respondent's cognitive functions through the use of headings and various visual coding techniques. Color coding a section to be completed, for example, reduces the required finding time for an item or group of items in the form by one-half. A respondent might be instructed to complete the "red" section for quickly highlighting the areas responsible for the complaint. Quick reference to this color-coded item saves time in searching among the form items. Hammer and Seymour (1965) found that time to locate an item increases linearly as a function of number of items in an array. The locating time for coded items (such as colored, bold print, and in italics), however, does not appreciably increase when increasing the number

FIGURE 4.2
A form configuration and layout illustrating human-factors design principles.

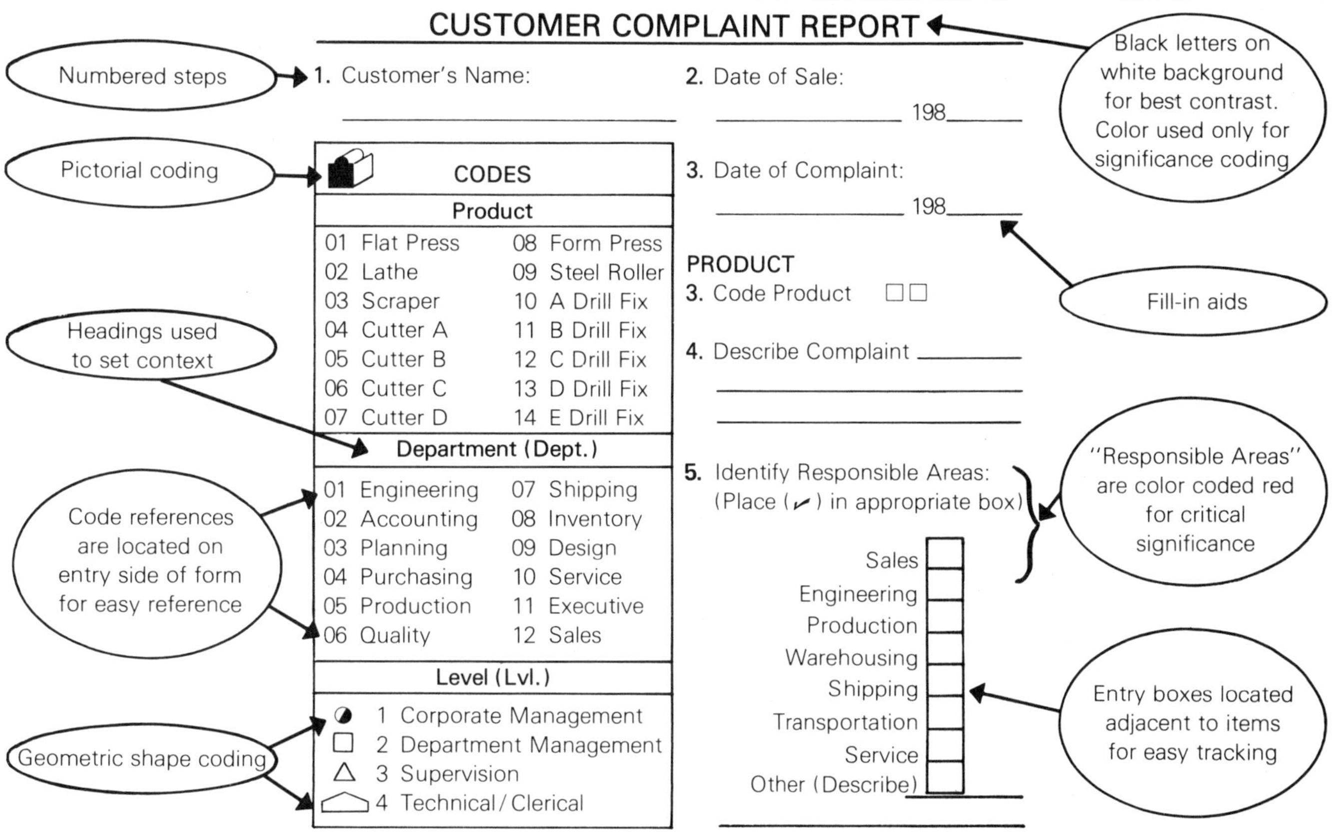

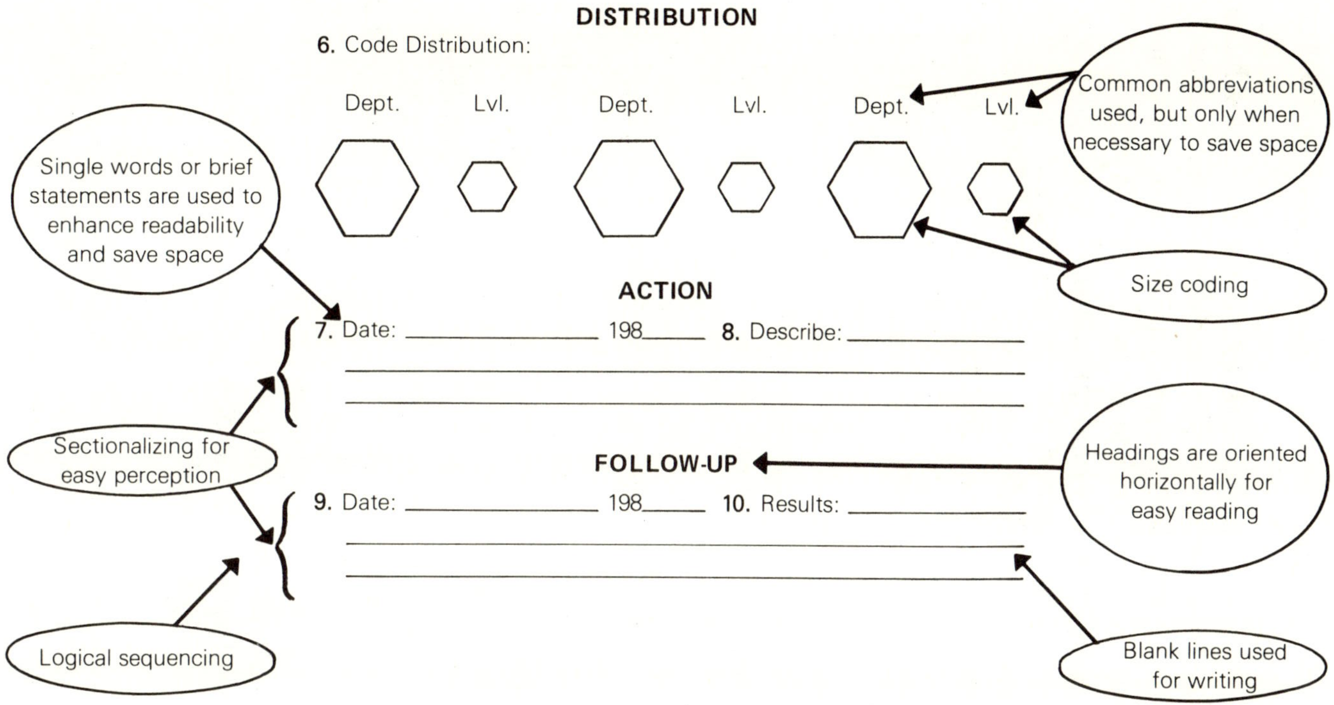
DISTRIBUTION
6. Code Distribution:
Dept.
Lvl.
Dept.
Lvl.
Dept.
Lvl.
ACTION
7. Date: 198
8. Describe:
FOLLOW-UP
9. Date: 198
10. Results:
Single words or brief statements are used to enhance readability and save space
Sectionalizing for easy perception
Logical sequencing
Common abbreviations used, but only when necessary to save space
Size coding
Headings are oriented horizontally for easy reading
Blank lines used for writing

of items. Coding yields up to as much as 70 percent time saving in item location.[1]

Readability is also enhanced in the illustrated format. The sequences are arranged logically, describing the product and the complaint, the responsible areas, the proposed distribution, the action to be taken and, later, the follow-up. Sections are easily read through perceptual grouping. When questions are scattered in the layout, much more time is required to locate an item. A scattered format would take about twice as much time to complete as the organized format in figure 4.2

When a respondent is required to turn the form over to find information on the reverse side, completion time is increased by about six seconds for each separate reference. Thus a respondent saves time repeatedly with code references on the same side as illustrated in figure 4.2.

Entries can be efficiently completed in the illustrated form design. Maximal use of space is provided by small margins and brief or single-word statements. Write-in spaces are of sufficient size for easy entry, and completion by hand or typewriter is facilitated when entry spaces are to the right or below the item where the hand or typewriter roller will not obscure the item to be read.

The inclusion of completion aids when possible also permits additional time saving. In figure 4.2, "198__" is used for the year, requiring only that the last digit be filled in. In other cases, circling a month or day could also reduce fill-in time. Computer-processed complaints would also permit automatic filling in of the customer's name, the date of sale, and the date of complaint, further reducing fill-in requirements.

---

1. Hammer and Seymour's study employed bold type for alphanumeric characters, as a kind of size coding. The same principle of coding operates when differential colors, shapes, or locations are used.

SUMMARY

Proper configuration and layout can result in reliable and accurate information to be derived from a form, while reducing the fill-in time to a minimum. The application of human-engineering principles can enhance the recognition and readability of the form and its elements and provide for efficient and convenient responses. The use of headings and various types of visual coding can greatly improve the respondent's recognition of the form and its components. Readability is markedly enhanced by the use of certain print dimensions and style and by logical sequencing and grouping of form content. Execution of form entries is most efficient when fill-in spaces are adequate and entry points are efficiently designed. The proper orientation of form instructions and references also contribute to forms-completion efficiency.

CHAPTER 5

Designing Forms Fill-In Instructions

Good writing is generally defined by conventional rules of syntax and grammar. Now, however, empirical data are also available on the kind of language that people can best understand, either in their profession (Tichy, 1966) or when called upon to fill out forms.

Effective writing techniques for designing forms fill-in instructions depend on the background and occupations of the respondents involved, the kinds of forms being considered, and the way in which the fill-in instructions will be used, for example, are they to be read only once or are they to be used as a reference or information source (Melby et al., 1977). Fill-in instructions for simple forms can be unnecessarily complex and tedious, creating confusion and irritating the respondents. Direct and uncomplicated instructions not only are best suited to the times but also elicit responses most efficiently (*Human Factors Bulletin*, 1979). Complex instructions, however necessary, result in increased work for the respondent. If the instructions are cumbersome, the respondent will perform poorly, and the effectiveness of the form can be severely degraded (Moray, 1979).

Ideally, form items to be filled in should be self-evident. Required instructional materials can only add to the cost and introduce interpretational variables that complicate the reliability of information. However, a questionnaire may of necessity be so complex that ancillary instructions must be provided. In such a case, the instructions must be designed to be clearly understood and accepted by the respondent.

Analytical Approach

A human-factors approach to the design of fill-in instruction is outlined in figure 5.1. In the forms design, minimum complexity is the first requirement in order to reduce instructional needs. Then a forms review is undertaken to determine how the form should be explained and where item clarification is needed. An instructions outline is developed and alternative methods of instruction are considered. A respondent population study is made to establish criteria for reading-level design. Reading comprehension development involves incorporating readability principles into the instructional material design. Finally, evaluation and revision of the instructions are completed on a rational basis and through empirical tests.

Forms Review

In studying the form, its purpose, general organization, and item-by-item meaning may become evident. If not, and if the form cannot be simplified, specific points where explanation is required must be ascertained.

FIGURE 5.1
A human-factors approach to the development of forms fill-in instructions.

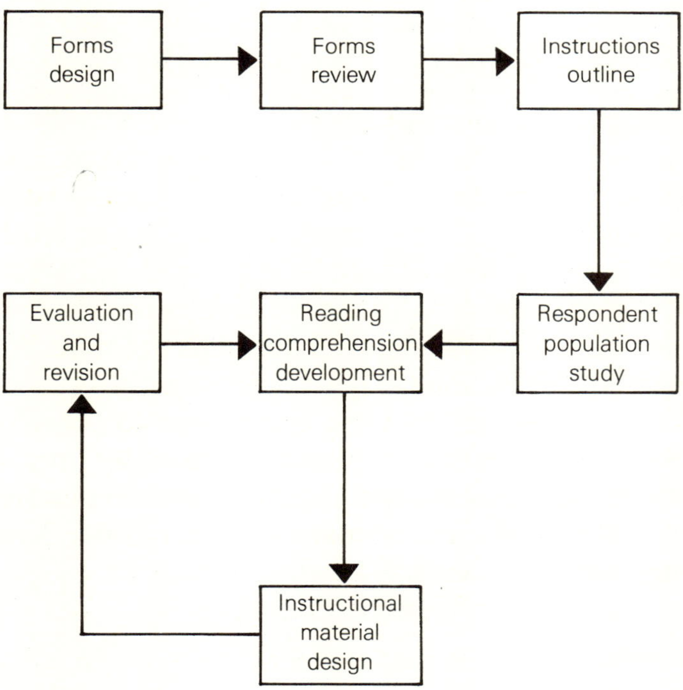

Preliminary design questions should include:

1. What does the respondent need to know about the purpose and overall use of the form? Could the form itself incorporate this information?
2. Is each form item self-explanatory or does it require further explanation? Could it be simplified? If not, could the clarification be carried on the form itself without overloading the format?
3. What are the minimal explanations and instructions needed to support the form?

The review should be completed and judgments made about required explanations and instructions not only by the forms-design staff but also by members of the respondent population. In fact, the latter can present the most valid case for needed instructions, since both the form and instructions are being designed for their use.

Instructions Outline

Following the review, the general outline of fill-in instructions can be completed. This might include a general orientation to use of the form and an outline of the instructions needed for each item.

Respondent Population Study

Instructional materials must take into account the characteristics and reading competence of the respondent population. Questions that must be answered for instructional materials design include the following:

1. What is the educational level of the respondent population (minimum to maximum grade levels completed)?
2. What is the technical competency of the respondents, and how much jargon do they understand?
3. What is the reading-grade level to be employed in instructions-material design? (The minimum expected level of reading competency should be employed rather

than the average or middle level of competency—which would exclude the lower 50 percent in comprehension.)

4. What word-usage standards should be incorporated in the design (syllables per word and number of words per sentence)?

READING COMPREHENSION DEVELOPMENT

In undertaking design of the fill-in instructions, the respondents' basic comprehension must be taken into consideration (Chall, 1948; Solomon and Postman, 1952; Klare, 1974; Lintz, 1979). Since the largest number of readers must understand the material most easily, the instructions writer should choose simple, familiar words. The words can be classified by their sources of learning in a person's life as follows:

1. Words learned before schooling began.
2. Words learned in elementary school.
3. Words learned from subjects in school or from hobbies and special interests.
4. Words learned from general language study and usage, such as idioms.
5. Slang expressions.
6. Foreign language word derivatives.
7. Words learned in special job training on equipment and its nomenclatures.

Earliest words learned are the most used. The child first learns to communicate to satisfy physical and emotional needs and becomes thoroughly familiar with these first word meanings. Early words are short, of few syllables, and predominantly have only one meaning (for example, take, open, ask, go, come, hot, cold, put, see, down, small, big, found, lost).

Combinations of basic words expand the world of the child, for example, "Go in the house." This is a phrase learned before the child attended school. A person may learn the term "ingress" later in school, but he never forgets what "go in" means. Words learned later in life, if not used frequently, are often forgotten. On seeing them again in written instructions, the respondent might have to relearn them.

Special words are learned in specific subjects in school or in hobbies or on projects. Such words should be used only for a reader who has a similar education and the same interests as the writer. Using such words limits the number of respondents who can easily understand the writing. In preparing fill-in instructions, the writer must translate technical terms to familiar words the reader can understand and act on. When the concept is complicated, it may require both words and illustrations to explain.

Words used in the development of forms instructions may be safely drawn from the preschool and elementary school levels. These would most likely be best understood by almost all respondents. Many idioms are also learned as part of the basic vocabulary. Idiomatic expressions could, therefore, be used where applicable. Precise meanings are possible with idioms, such as "Turn on the switch" rather than "Energize the circuit."

Slang should be avoided, since it is peculiar to specific times and geographic areas. Slang may also be offensive to some respondents and thus detract from the effectiveness of the form. Words of foreign-language origin should also be avoided, since respondents may lack the necessary language background.

Words learned from working with given equipment or systems should be used carefully and only if understood in the common work context. Also, equipment designations should be written exactly as they appear on equipment or in documents—with the same spacing, spelling, abbreviations, and the like.

Phrasing

The manner in which instructions are phrased can also influence a respondent's comprehension. The proper use of subordinate clauses and appropriate sentence structures and active and negative statements are important to understanding.

Subordinate Clauses

Complex sentences are most easily understood if the subordinate clause is introduced by a relative pronoun. "The machine drill *that* the customer complained about had broken" is clearer than "The machine drill the customer complained about." If a relative pronoun is not used, the reader might infer a conjunction or verb that would change the meaning. The relative pronoun fixes the relationship and prevents inadvertent meaning changes (Cherry, 1961; Blumenthal, 1966).

Sentence Structure

Though short sentences are generally recommended, closely interrelated meanings are more readily grasped when presented in the same sentence. In a study (Bradford and Franks, 1971), readers were presented with the sentences: "The dog chased the cat. The dog was black. the cat was ginger." These short sentences were later recalled as, "The black dog chased the ginger cat." Complex sentences are more easily understood than short sentences when the meanings are related. However, it is important to keep clauses relatively short, and to limit their number within a sentence.

Mood and Voice

When instructions involve direct action, the imperative mood, "Return the invoice to the sender," is preferable to the indirect command, "The invoice should be returned to the sender." Use of the active or passive voice is determined by the emphasis desired, for example, "The government applied the regulations" (active) or "Regulations were applied" (passive). In the first instance, government is emphasized, and in the second, the regulations are given emphasis (Goldman-Eisler and Cohen, 1970; Ansfeld and Klenbort, 1973).

The Use of Negatives

Negative statements may be effective in correcting erroneous assumptions of a reader. "Do not use a pencil when completing this form" is more effective than "Complete this form in ink." The affirmative statement may be construed by a respondent as merely a preference by the administration rather than a fundamental requirement. Respondents more accurately follow instructions, in some situations, if negatives are used to reinforce a negative emphasis. Johnson and Altman (1973) found that passenger behavior on aircraft-evacuation slide chutes became significantly more efficient when "JUMP—DON'T SIT" was provided in card instructions, compared with simply "JUMP." Where a negative emphasis is not needed, however, the use of a negative is of little value.

Write and Rewrite

Clarity generally does not occur in the first writing. Almost any descriptive text can be improved by careful examination and editing. Rewriting may be necessary to make the material more respondent oriented and more understandable. First writings may contain slang and colloquialisms that are offensive to some readers or they may lack objectivity and empathy. In subsequent writings, more concern for the reader may become evident through increasing clarity. Consider the following difficult instructions concerning withholding tax from the IRS income-tax manual:

Excess FIAC and RRTA Tax Withheld—Two or More Employers
If you had two or more employers... who together paid you more than $29,700 in wages, too much social security tax (FIAC) and railroad retirement tax (RRTA) may have been withheld from your wages. If so, you may be able to take credit for it against your income tax. If any one employer withheld more than $1975.05, you should ask the employer to refund the excess to you. You cannot take credit for it on your return.

These instructions might be rewritten as follows:

A single employer deducts up to $1975.05 in retirement tax when you earn more than $29,700 in wages. Recover amounts deducted in excess of $1975.05 from the employer. If more than one employer is involved, and more than $1975.05 is deducted for retirement tax, apply the excess amount as credit on your income tax.

Rewriting this explanation a number of times, while carefully considering the respondent's point of view, could result in increasing clarity.

As a general principle, long sentences can often be shortened to improve clarity. Rather than using sentences that employ a string of conjunctions, for example, item fill-in conditions could be listed as follows:

Complete section 13 if the following applies:

1. You are over 18 years of age.
2. You have been a resident of the United States since your last birthday.
3. Your parents do not reside in the United States.
4. You have not been claimed as a financial dependent by any persons filing income tax.

Designing the Instructions

A number of different methods and formats can be considered in the design of fill-in instructions. These include printed flowcharts, tabular procedural outlines, and the use of pictorial aids (Blaiwes, 1974; Kammann, 1975; Gade et al., 1981).

Flowcharts. One alternative to narrative fill-in instructions is the use of a flowchart. Figure 5.2 illustrates a flowchart diagraming instructions for the forms to be used to obtain facilities-design information. Such flowcharts are most effectively used when a great many potentially irrelevant factors operate; flow paths in the chart can eliminate them. The format is also appropriate in displaying different circumstances that require different sets of questions (Wright and Reid, 1973).

Tabular Formats. When narrative directions are not sufficiently concise in conveying complex instructions, tabular formats may be used. The tabular format is effective in supplying step-by-step instructional information to a respondent (Wiedman and Ireland, 1965; Haney, 1969). Haney employed a tabular format when it became apparent through testing that a narrative format did not provide the information as readily as a tabular format. Results indicated that the technicians using narrative manuals make three times as many errors as those using tabular formats and that the latter could spend 5 percent more time in testing, per se.

Figure 5.3 presents a tabular format of the analytical processes for deriving environmental design data. This provides guidelines for a building user for completing information on interior design requirements. Listed under *Reading Needs Type* are areas for design control, the specifics of which are iterated under the heading *Design-Requirements Information.* Each specific item serves as a stimulus for the respondent. Under the heading *Acceptable Verification* the responses must be coordinated with those of other respondents or physical measurements obtained to verify the requirements information. Deviations from the format are indicated under the heading *Exceptions.*

FIGURE 5.2
An illustrative instructional flow chart for determining appropriate engineering forms.

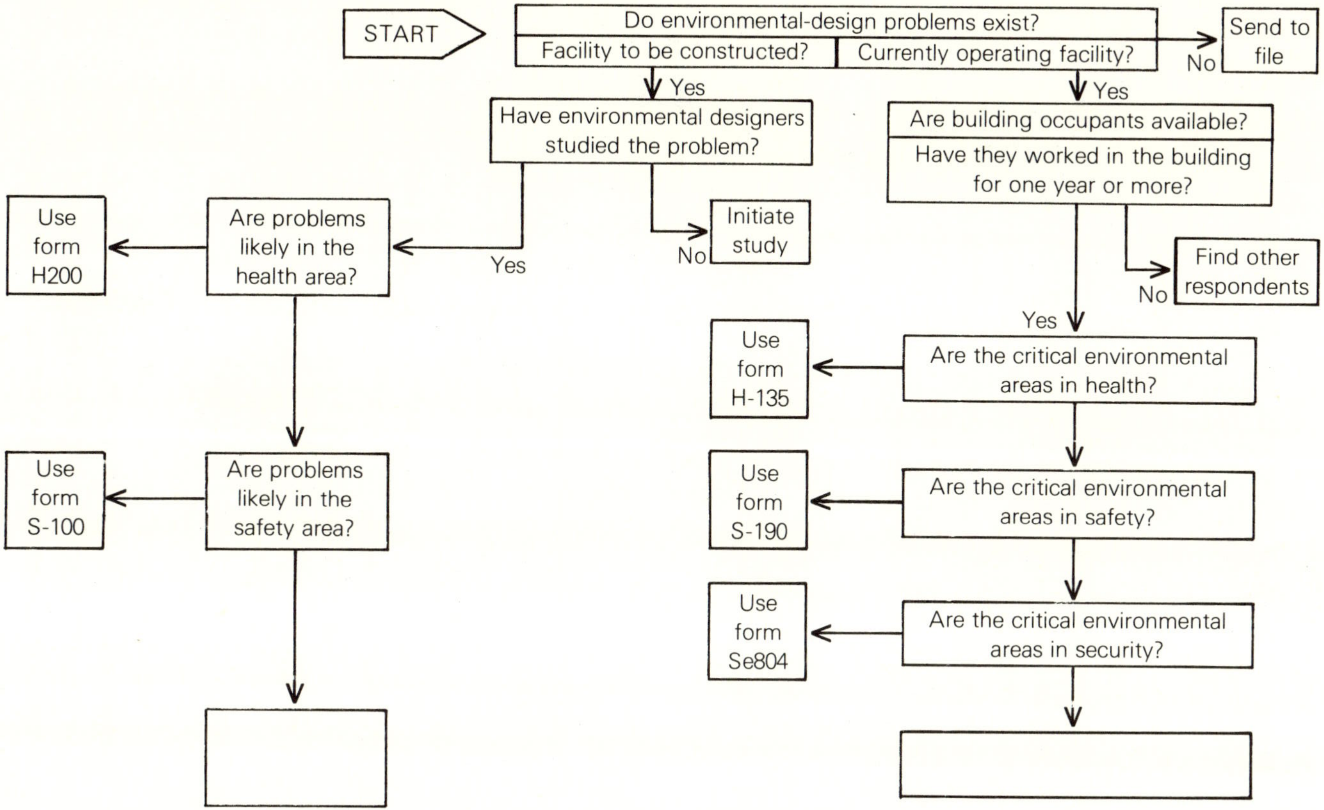

FIGURE 5.3
An illustrative tabular format of instructions for compiling engineering information.

Deriving Environmental-Design Data

Needs Type	Design-Requirements Information	Acceptable Verification	Exceptions
Health	Air or atmospheric control	1. Descriptive data from at least two out of three independent sources	Indicate where requirement does not apply
	Temperature control, normal and extreme	2. Instrumented measures	Cite additional requirements not covered
	Infectious disease control	3. Questionnaire data developed from representative population	
	Sound-level control		
	Lighting, glare, and flash control		
	Toilet and waste control		
	Cleaning and custodial maintenance		
Safety	Mechanical hazard control		

Figure 5.4 shows a tabular restructuring of instructions for itemized interest deductions taken from the U.S. Internal Revenue Service income-tax instructions.

The problem in using other than narrative instructions is the novel and unfamiliar aspect of the alternative formats. A general respondent population may be intimidated by a flowchart or tabular presentation. When such devices are introduced, it is always advisable to test the instructions on a small sample from the relevant population of users.

Pictorial Aids

Pictorial, graphic, or other visual aids can be useful. Studies on comprehension of tax regulations and operating instructions for telephones indicate that only 60 to 75 percent of the readers understood the directions. However, when respondents are provided with visual aids, there is a significant improvement in understanding (Kammann, 1975). This improvement varies with the nature of the material, the characteristics of the respondent population, and the complexity and length of the form.

Printed Text

Mechanical printing requirements for good readability are described in chapter 4. Narrow columns of print, like those in newspapers, allow a reader to scan vertically without the need for a return sweep of the eyes. Reading studies based on number of eye fixations indicate reading advantages in double spacing and increasing the density of print from thirty-five characters per line to seventy (Kolers et al., 1980; 1981). Although these studies involved print on cathode-ray tubes, the implications may be valid for printed forms fill-in instructions.

The slight advantage of double spacing, where more words were read per fixation, may be offset by the increased space required.

FIGURE 5.4
A tabular information structure alternative to the IRS narrative format.

Itemized Deductions (Cont.)

Item	What to do	Interest Deductable	Interest Not Deductable
Interest expense	Add up deductable interest charges. Enter total on Line 20 of Schedule A	1. Home mortgage 2. Credit card 3. Revolving charge account 4. Personal note loans 5. Life-insurance loans 6. Installment contracts 7. Late taxes (excluding penalty) 8. Investment-property loans	1. Tax-exempt income 2. Life-insurance loans when interest is added to the loan 3. Loans used to buy single-premium life insurance or endowment contract 4. Business loans (Use Schedules CE or F)

See Publication 545

Doubling the number of characters per line by reducing their size increases the number of visual fixations per line from 4.8 to 8.0. However, the number of words acquired with each fixation increases, hence the overall reading time is decreased.

EVALUATION AND REVIEW

A review of the literature on readability reveals that many instructional documents are written beyond the level of good respondent comprehension (Norcott, 1975; Kilty, 1976). An evaluation of reading difficulty was completed for a number of different materials using the Dale-Chall readability formula described in the 1948 *Educational Research Bulletin.* These materials included the official State of Michigan driver's manual, a small-claims court claims form, federal income tax instructions, the Michigan Social Service unemployment and food-stamp application forms, and instructions for completing the national health insurance application. Reading levels of difficulty for these materials ranged from seventh grade through college level.

None of the materials was designed to correspond with the reading level of the using population. For example, food-stamp application instructions were written at an eleventh-grade reading level. The national health insurance application required a college reading-level capability. The reading-difficulty levels of most of the materials studied were beyond the ability of the readership for whom they were intended. An earlier study of U.S. Navy publications also indicated that training and instructional materials were written at far too high a level for the personnel using the manuals (Stanlee and Fattu, 1956).

Rational Assessment of Reading-Level Difficulty

Good design of forms fill-in instructions requires careful correlation of the reading-level difficulty with the reading skill of the respondent populations. For example, based on respondent-population characteristics, it might be determined that a ninth-grade level of reading difficulty should be used.

Rational assessment of instructions material can be accomplished through the use of a reading-difficulty formula. A commonly used formula is the Flesch Reading Ease Score (FRES). FRES employs measures of word difficulty and sentence length to assess readability (Flesch, 1948). Word difficulty is a measure of the average number of syllables per word. Sentence length is the average number of words per sentence. The syllable measures may be made using a stylus counter. The syllables are pronounced while the stylus-actuated counter is depressed to obtain a count of each syllable tallied per word. Words per sentence can be counted directly. The reading level is then determined by averaging syllables per word and words per sentence (Smith and Kincaid, 1970; Kincaid and Delionback, 1973; Gamble and Kincaid, 1976; Biersner and Bunde, 1979).

Empirical Assessment

The use of readability formulas for assessment should be supplemented with empirical testing. A readability formula normally does not measure conceptual difficulty, as this can best be measured by testing a sample of respondents. Their general opinion of the instructional material can be useful, but more quantitative techniques are also required. A conceptual-evaluation method commonly used is the Gates-MacGinite form F test, also called the "Cloze" procedure. In this procedure, form fill-in instructions are prepared with every fifth word left blank. If all of the sampled respondents can fill in 35 percent or more of the blanks, the instructions are deemed to be understandable. If more than 10 percent of the respondents score under 35 percent, the instructions are considered too difficult and should be rewritten.

SUMMARY

Designing instructions for forms to be filled in requires care to assure respondent understanding. Instructional materials are often written at unappropriate reading levels, thus compromising the effectiveness of the material.

The use of familiar words is recommended. Principles and specifics of writing for good understanding are described. Flow charts and tabular formats are considered as alternatives to conventional prose in the preparation of instructions. Reading and conceptual levels require evaluation when refining the instructions. The designer should be primarily concerned with the respondents' understanding throughout the preparation of instructional materials.

CHAPTER 6

An Evaluation of Some Common Government Forms

The government agencies that issue forms are bureaucracies, dedicated to the routines of government, and implicitly opposed to innovative changes such as improvements in forms and practices (Dyer and Dyer, 1969). Yet the government is the greatest bulk producer of forms used in regulating and taxing individuals and businesses.

As citizens and entrepreneurs we seem to be without recourse, and we appeal in vain to government agencies to lighten our administrative burden. Forms, it appears, must be designed strictly at agency discretion. We are obliged only to return them promptly, filled out accurately and completely.

Government agencies and private entrepreneurs differ radically in their perception of the problem. The strong desire of the private sector for forms improvement stems from a cost-saving and profit-making orientation. Government agencies, in contrast, grow and prosper when forms are so complex and unwieldy that they require expansion of the work force.

General operational differences between businesses and government bureaucracies are outlined in table 6.1 (Weber, 1947; Bendix, 1957; Strauss, 1961; Burgess, 1978). It can be seen that private entrepreneurs are fundamentally receptive to innovative and cost-saving ideas by virtue of their organizational goals and missions. A government agency, on the other hand, is relatively indifferent to cost-saving appeals because financial survival is assured by a stable tax base. Reliance of the government agency on internal interdependencies also makes it somewhat immune to outside influences. Any individual initiatives within the bureaucratic organization to improve forms design may also be subject to priorities of immediate supervisors within the hierarchy. Individual bureaucrats may find that forms improvement often depends on the discretion and prejudices of a superior. This sometimes results in stifling the initiative of the individual bureaucrat, who, in turn, may react in a similar fashion to prevent his subordinates from undertaking design improvements (Strauss, 1961; Burgess, 1970). The universality of rules within the hierarchy and the insistence on order in government departments seem better suited to keeping the status quo than militating for their improvement.

The strength of governmental agencies or bureaucracies as Max Weber observed them lies in their excellence of organization. Weber likened bureaucratic operation to machine production, yielding precision, speed, knowledge of files, continuity, discretion, unity, strict subordination, and minimized friction. Such functional characteristics operate in an optimal fashion within bureaucratic organizations.[1]

1. For a discussion of Weber's point of view on bureaucratic excellence, refer to Reinhard Bendix's book, *Max Weber, An Intellectual Portrait* (New York: Doubleday, 1960), p. 421.

TABLE 6.1 (continued)
An operational comparison of private business versus government bureaucracy.

Operational Characteristic	Business	Government Agency
Authority	A one-man authority predominates, which is predicated on making things happen.	Rules predominate, which are predicated on making things orderly.
Products or services	The organization is oriented toward selling goods or services to outsiders. Customer acceptance is the primary concern.	The agency is oriented toward maintaining routines and impressing insiders to gain their approbation.
Response priority	The organization reacts primarily to external stimuli. It relates its actions to the customer needs.	The organization reacts primarily to internal stimuli, preparing reports and keeping records for the approbation of superiors.
Flexibility	Routines and assignments are readily varied to provide improved service to outsiders.	Routines are largely inflexible.
Attitude toward outsiders	Outsider is accepted as a necessity.	Outsider is resented as an annoyance.

TABLE 6.1
An operational comparison of private business versus government bureaucracy.

Operational Characteristic	Business	Government Agency
Leadership	Entrepreneur must exploit the market to achieve financial success. Subordinates contribute to financial success in following the same precept.	A subordinate's position is secured by pleasing the person above him.
Ownership	Resources are owned by the management, stockholders, or private entrepreneur.	The operation is supported by taxation. Resources are not owned by the officials; they are only held accountable.
Rewards and incentive	Money and power are sought through effective production and marketing.	Regular salary advancement is achieved through lifetime career patterns.
Growth	An increased work volume requires additional workers and administrative controls to prevent excessive fiscal expenditures.	New procedures and services introduce an increasing number of tasks that require specialists and additional layers of administrators.
Job status	The person is rewarded on the basis of competence and performance. Lines of authority are clear cut. Promotion is made when the person contributes to financial success or prestige of the organization.	Job is paid for on a career-system basis. Promotion is made by a superior, or on seniority.

IMPROVING GOVERNMENT FORMS

If design improvements are to be incorporated into government forms, the bureaucratic structure and its operational priorities must first be considered. An individual agency, for example, might turn a deaf ear to complaints about forms design unless proposed design changes are related to internal agency problems or unless political muscle can be exerted to bring about needed improvements.

Direct Benefits to the Agency

Improvements to forms issued by government agencies must be related, at the outset, directly to agency benefits. In its bureaucratic character, an agency is primarily concerned with maintaining internal efficiency, in capturing, processing, and reporting information. When it can be demonstrated that a form's design fails to achieve such efficiency, design changes may be more readily incorporated.

Strategies to Achieve Respondent Benefits

Unwieldy agency forms that are foisted on the citizenry are often responsible for a deluge of paperwork about which individuals and businesses complain. Specific complaints and recommended improvements can often be made politically through elected officials. Elected officials, when pressured by their constituents, are generally responsive and can often exert sufficient influence to bring about form changes within the bureaucracies. Political pressure was no doubt responsible for passage of the Paperwork Reduction Act of 1980, which now requires an agency to inform respondents why the form information is required, how it will be used, and if the requirement is without appeal. Respondents can emphatically benefit from improved forms design through easier comprehension of the form, and shortened fill-in time.

Design and Evaluation of Government Forms

A cross section of government forms-design programs, and several forms used for taxing and regulatory purposes, are presented in this chapter. The common government forms selected for evaluation include U.S. income tax and postal service forms, and New York State driver licensing and automobile registration application forms.

FEDERAL GOVERNMENT FORMS

The General Services Administration (GSA) provides guidance to other federal agencies on forms design. While each agency has its own forms-management program, the GSA provides a forms-management consulting service and is responsible for helping federal agencies improve their program performance through effective, economical, and efficient records management. The GSA also assists the agencies in the design and installation of forms.

GSA has developed handbooks for use by federal agencies on forms-management programs. A comprehensive two-week course is given periodically on forms analysis and design for the agencies, management analysts, and forms designers. GSA also contracts with outside consulting firms to obtain additional forms-design expertise.[2]

The Internal Revenue Service (IRS) conducts an ongoing forms-improvement program for all the tax forms it issues. Changes in the tax laws and regulations by the Congress are continually enacted and require yearly forms revisions. The

---

2. GSA information is based on a phone conversation, August 18, 1979, with Donald Hansen, chief of forms management, General Services Administration, and on correspondence dated August 23, 1978, with James Rhoads, archivist of the United States National Archives and Records Service, Washington, D.C.

major problem in tax forms design is to find the space to incorporate these revisions.[3]

In the IRS forms-improvement program, an attempt is made to meet with the public and the IRS field office personnel in order to learn where the forms problems are. An internal IRS tax forms coordinating committee reviews all proposed forms changes and decides on those to be implemented.

Forms Improvement

Appendix B outlines the human-factors principles in forms design against which different forms can be evaluated. In reviewing IRS Form 1040 against these human-factors standards, it can be seen that only a few improvements have been made in the five-year period from 1977 to 1982. Between 1977 and 1978, horizontal printing was introduced for instructions on attaching the W-2 form and check or money order (exhibits A and B). Redundant instructions for attaching the W-2 form were also deleted in 1978. Other revisions of the 1040 form were primarily a result of changes in the tax laws, such as items 15 and 31.

Form 1040

A more recent Form 1040 is illustrated in exhibit C. Information items included on the form are judged by designers to be only those necessary to ensure compliance with the tax laws, and enable the individual to compute and pay the right amount of income tax.

Content. Only single words or brief sentences are used in this form. The active voice is employed on all items, though

3. Background information on the IRS forms program was obtained in a phone conversation August 24, 1978, with Len Caracciolo, Forms Management, Internal Revenue Service.

EXHIBIT A

U.S. Form 1040, 1977 Income Tax Summary

Form **1040** Department of the Treasury—Internal Revenue Service **U.S. Individual Income Tax Return 1977**

For the year January 1–December 31, 1977, or other taxable year beginning 1977 ending , 19

Use IRS label. Otherwise, print or type.

First name and initial (if joint return, give first names and initials of both) | Last name | Your social security number

Present home address (Number and street, including apartment number, or rural route) | For Privacy Act Notice, see page 3 of Instructions. | Spouse's social security no.

City, town or post office, State and ZIP code | Occupation: Yours ▶ Spouse's ▶

Presidential Election Campaign Fund ▶ Do you want $1 to go to this fund? . . . Yes No
If joint return, does your spouse want $1 to go to this fund? . Yes No

Note: *Checking "Yes" will not increase your tax or reduce your refund.*

Filing Status — Check Only One Box
1 Single
2 Married filing joint return (even if only one had income)
3 Married filing separately. If spouse is also filing, give spouse's social security number in the space above and enter full name here ▶
4 Unmarried Head of Household. Enter qualifying name ▶ See page 7 of Instructions.
5 Qualifying widow(er) with dependent child (Year spouse died ▶ 19). See page 7 of Instructions.

Exemptions — Always check the "Yourself" box. Check other boxes if they apply.
6a Yourself 65 or over Blind
b Spouse 65 or over Blind — Enter number of boxes checked on 6a and b ▶
c First names of your dependent children who lived with you ▶ — Enter number of children listed ▶

d Other dependents: (1) Name	(2) Relationship	(3) Number of months lived in your home.	(4) Did dependent have income of $750 or more?	(5) Did you provide more than one-half of dependent's support?

Enter number of other dependents ▶

7 Total number of exemptions claimed . . . Add numbers entered in boxes above ▶

Please Attach Copy B of Forms W-2 Here

Income
8 Wages, salaries, tips, and other employee compensation. (Attach Forms W-2. If unavailable, see page 5 of Instructions.) . . . 8
9 Interest income. (If over $400, attach Schedule B.) . . . 9
10a Dividends (If over $400, attach Schedule B) ...., 10b less exclusion ...., Balance ▶ 10c
(See pages 9 and 17 of Instructions)
(If you have no other income, **skip** *lines 11 through 20 and go to line 21.)*
11 State and local income tax refunds (does not apply if refund is for year you took standard deduction) . . . 11
12 Alimony received . . . 12
13 Business income or (loss) (attach Schedule C) . . . 13
14 Capital gain or (loss) (attach Schedule D) . . . 14
15 50% of capital gain distributions not reported on Schedule D . . . 15
16 Net gain or (loss) from Supplemental Schedule of Gains and Losses (attach Form 4797) . . 16
17 Fully taxable pensions and annuities not reported on Schedule E . . . 17
18 Pensions, annuities, rents, royalties, partnerships, estates or trusts, etc. (attach Schedule E) . 18
19 Farm income or (loss) (attach Schedule F) . . . 19
20 Other (state nature and source—see page 9 of Instructions) ▶ 20
21 **Total income.** Add lines 8, 9, and 10c through 20 . . . ▶ 21

Please Attach Check or Money Order Here

Adjustments to Income *(If none,* **skip** *lines 22 through 27 and enter zero on line 28.)*
22 Moving expense (attach Form 3903) . . . 22
23 Employee business expenses (attach Form 2106) . . . 23
24 Payments to an individual retirement arrangement (from attached Form 5329, Part III) . . . 24
25 Payments to a Keogh (H.R. 10) retirement plan . . . 25
26 Forfeited interest penalty for premature withdrawal . . . 26
27 Alimony paid (see page 11 of Instructions) . . . 27
28 **Total adjustments.** Add lines 22 through 27 . . . ▶ 28
29 Subtract line 28 from line 21 . . . 29
30 Disability income exclusion (sick pay) (attach Form 2440) . . . 30
31 **Adjusted gross income.** Subtract line 30 from line 29. Enter here and on line 32. If you want IRS to figure your tax for you, see page 4 of the Instructions . . . ▶ 31

EXHIBIT B
U.S. Form 1040, 1978 Income Tax Summary

Form **1040** Department of the Treasury—Internal Revenue Service
U.S. Individual Income Tax Return **1978**

For Privacy Act Notice, see page 3 of Instructions | For the year January 1–December 31, 1978, or other tax year beginning 1978, ending 19

Use IRS label. Otherwise, please print or type.	Your first name and initial (if joint return, also give spouse's name and initial)	Last name	Your social security number
	Present home address (Number and street, including apartment number, or rural route)		Spouse's social security no.
	City, town or post office, State and ZIP code		Your occupation

Do you want $1 to go to the Presidential Election Campaign Fund? Yes No
If joint return, does your spouse want $1 to go to this fund? . . Yes No
Note: *Checking Yes will not increase your tax or reduce your refund.*
Spouse's occupation

Filing Status
Check only one box.
1 Single
2 Married filing joint return (even if only one had income)
3 Married filing separate return. If spouse is also filing, give spouse's social security number in the space above and enter full name here ▶
4 Unmarried head of household. Enter qualifying name ▶ ______. See page 6 of Instructions.
5 Qualifying widow(er) with dependent child (Year spouse died ▶ 19). See page 6 of Instructions.

Exemptions
Always check the box labeled Yourself. Check other boxes if they apply.
6a Yourself 65 or over Blind
b Spouse 65 or over Blind
Enter number of boxes checked on 6a and b ▶
c First names of your dependent children who lived with you ▶
Enter number of children listed ▶

d Other dependents: (1) Name	(2) Relationship	(3) Number of months lived in your home	(4) Did dependent have income of $750 or more?	(5) Did you provide more than one-half of dependent's support?

Enter number of other dependents ▶
7 Total number of exemptions claimed . . . . Add numbers entered in boxes above ▶

Income
Please attach Copy B of your Forms W-2 here.
If you do not have a W-2, see page 5 of Instructions.
Please attach check or money order here.

8	Wages, salaries, tips, and other employee compensation	8
9	Interest income *(If over $400, attach Schedule B)*	9
10a	Dividends *(If over $400, attach Schedule B)* ______, 10b Exclusion ______	
10c	Subtract line 10b from line 10a	10c
11	State and local income tax refunds *(does not apply unless refund is for year you itemized deductions)*	11
12	Alimony received	12
13	Business income or (loss) *(attach Schedule C)*	13
14	Capital gain or (loss) *(attach Schedule D)*	14
15	Taxable part of capital gain distributions not reported on Schedule D (see page 9 of Instructions) . .	15
16	Net gain or (loss) from Supplemental Schedule of Gains and Losses *(attach Form 4797)*	16
17	Fully taxable pensions and annuities not reported on Schedule E	17
18	Pensions, annuities, rents, royalties, partnerships, estates or trusts, etc. *(attach Schedule E)*	18
19	Farm income or (loss) *(attach Schedule F)*	19
20	Other income (state nature and source—see page 10 of Instructions) ▶	20
21	**Total income.** Add lines 8, 9, and 10c through 20 . . . . . . ▶	21

Adjustments to Income

22	Moving expense *(attach Form 3903)*	22
23	Employee business expenses *(attach Form 2106)* . .	23
24	Payments to an IRA (see page 10 of Instructions)	24
25	Payments to a Keogh *(H.R. 10)* retirement plan . . .	25
26	Interest penalty due to early withdrawal of savings	26
27	Alimony paid (see page 10 of Instructions)	27
28	**Total adjustments.** Add lines 22 through 27 . . . . . . ▶	28

Adjusted Gross Income

29	Subtract line 28 from line 21	29
30	Disability income exclusion *(attach Form 2440)*	30
31	**Adjusted gross income.** Subtract line 30 from line 29. *If this line is less than $8,000, see page 2 of Instructions.* If you want IRS to figure your tax, see page 4 of Instructions . . . . . . ▶	31

Form 1040 (1978)

EXHIBIT C
U.S. Form 1040, 1981 Income Tax Summary

Form **1040** Department of the Treasury—Internal Revenue Service
U.S. Individual Income Tax Return **1981** (B)

For the year January 1–December 31, 1981, or other tax year beginning 1981, ending 19 | OMB No. 1545-0074

Use IRS label. Otherwise, please print or type.

Your first name and initial (if joint return, also give spouse's name and initial) | Last name | Your social security number
Present home address (Number and street, including apartment number, or rural route) | Spouse's social security no.
City, town or post office, State and ZIP code | Your occupation ▶ | Spouse's occupation ▶

Presidential Election Campaign ▶ Do you want $1 to go to this fund? . . . Yes No
If joint return, does your spouse want $1 to go to this fund? . . . Yes No
Note: Checking "Yes" will not increase your tax or reduce your refund.

For Privacy Act and Paperwork Reduction Act Notice, see Instructions.

Filing Status
Check only one box.

1 Single
2 Married filing joint return (even if only one had income)
3 Married filing separate return. Enter spouse's social security no. above and full name here ▶
4 Head of household (with qualifying person). (See page 6 of Instructions.) If he or she is your unmarried child, enter child's name ▶
5 Qualifying widow(er) with dependent child (Year spouse died ▶ 19). (See page 6 of Instructions.)

Exemptions
Always check the box labeled Yourself. Check other boxes if they apply.

6a Yourself | 65 or over | Blind
b Spouse | 65 or over | Blind
Enter number of boxes checked on 6a and b ▶
c First names of your dependent children who lived with you ▶
Enter number of children listed on 6c ▶

d Other dependents:

(1) Name	(2) Relationship	(3) Number of months lived in your home	(4) Did dependent have income of $1,000 or more?	(5) Did you provide more than one-half of dependent's support?

Enter number of other dependents ▶
e Total number of exemptions claimed . . . Add numbers entered in boxes above ▶

Income
Please attach Copy B of your Forms W-2 here.
If you do not have a W-2, see page 5 of Instructions.

7 Wages, salaries, tips, etc. . . . 7
8a Interest income (attach Schedule B if over $400 or you have any All-Savers interest) . . . 8a
b Dividends (attach Schedule B if over $400) . . . 8b
c Total. Add lines 8a and 8b . . . 8c
d Exclusion (See page 9 of Instructions) . . . 8d
e Subtract line 8d from line 8c (but not less than zero) . . . 8e
9 Refunds of State and local income taxes (do not enter an amount unless you deducted those taxes in an earlier year—see page 9 of Instructions) . . . 9
10 Alimony received . . . 10
11 Business income or (loss) (attach Schedule C) . . . ▶ 11
12 Capital gain or (loss) (attach Schedule D) . . . 12
13 40% of capital gain distributions not reported on line 12 (See page 9 of Instructions) . 13
14 Supplemental gains or (losses) (attach Form 4797) . . . 14
15 Fully taxable pensions and annuities not reported on line 16 . . . 15
16a Other pensions and annuities. Total received . . . 16a
b Taxable amount, if any, from worksheet on page 10 of Instructions . . . 16b
17 Rents, royalties, partnerships, estates, trusts, etc. (attach Schedule E) . . . 17
18 Farm income or (loss) (attach Schedule F) . . . ▶ 18
19a Unemployment compensation (insurance). Total received 19a
b Taxable amount, if any, from worksheet on page 10 of Instructions . . . 19b
20 Other income (state nature and source—see page 11 of Instructions) ▶ 20
21 **Total income.** Add amounts in column for lines 7 through 20 . . . ▶ 21

Please attach check or money order here.

Adjustments to Income
(See Instructions on page 11)

22 Moving expense (attach Form 3903 or 3903F) . . . 22
23 Employee business expenses (attach Form 2106) . . . 23
24 Payments to an IRA (enter code from page 11 ....) . 24
25 Payments to a Keogh (H.R. 10) retirement plan . . . 25
26 Interest penalty on early withdrawal of savings . . . 26
27 Alimony paid . . . 27
28 Disability income exclusion (attach Form 2440) . . . 28
29 Other adjustments—see page 12 ▶ 29
30 **Total adjustments.** Add lines 22 through 29 . . . ▶ 30

Adjusted Gross Income
31 **Adjusted gross income.** Subtract line 30 from line 21. *If this line is less than $10,000, see "Earned Income Credit" (line 57) on page 15 of Instructions. If you want IRS to figure your tax, see page 3 of Instructions* . . . ▶ 31

☆ U.S. GOVERNMENT PRINTING OFFICE: 1981—0-343-248 E.I.#13-2687299

EXHIBIT C (continued)
U.S. Form 1040, 1981, reverse side

Form 1040 (1981) Page 2

Tax Computation (See Instructions on page 12)

32a	Amount from line 31 *(adjusted gross income)*	32a	
32b	If you do not itemize deductions, enter zero. If you itemize, complete Schedule A (Form 1040) and enter the amount from Schedule A, line 41	32b	
	Caution: If you have unearned income and can be claimed as a dependent on your parent's return, check here ▶ ☐ and see page 12 of the Instructions. Also see page 12 of the Instructions if: ● *You are married filing a separate return and your spouse itemizes deductions, OR* ● *You file Form 4563, OR* ● *You are a dual-status alien.*		
32c	Subtract line 32b from line 32a	32c	
33	Multiply $1,000 by the total number of exemptions claimed on Form 1040, line 6e	33	
34	Taxable Income. Subtract line 33 from line 32c	34	
35	Tax. Enter tax here and check if from ☐ Tax Table, ☐ Tax Rate Schedule X, Y, or Z, ☐ Schedule D, ☐ Schedule G, or ☐ Form 4726	35	
36	Additional Taxes. (See page 13 of Instructions.) Enter here and check if from ☐ Form 4970, ☐ Form 4972, ☐ Form 5544, or ☐ Section 72(m)(5) penalty tax	36	
37	**Total.** Add lines 35 and 36 ▶	37	

Credits (See Instructions on page 13)

38	Credit for contributions to candidates for public office	38			
39	Credit for the elderly *(attach Schedules R&RP)*	39			
40	Credit for child and dependent care expenses *(attach Form 2441)*	40			
41	Investment credit *(attach Form 3468)*	41			
42	Foreign tax credit *(attach Form 1116)*	42			
43	Work incentive (WIN) credit *(attach Form 4874)*	43			
44	Jobs credit *(attach Form 5884)*	44			
45	Residential energy credit *(attach Form 5695)*	45			
46	**Total credits.** Add lines 38 through 45			46	
47	**Balance.** Subtract line 46 from line 37 and enter difference (but not less than zero) ▶			47	

Other Taxes (Including Advance EIC Payments)

48	Self-employment tax *(attach Schedule SE)*	48	
49a	Minimum tax. Attach Form 4625 and check here ▶ ☐	49a	
49b	Alternative minimum tax. Attach Form 6251 and check here ▶ ☐	49b	
50	Tax from recomputing prior-year investment credit *(attach Form 4255)*	50	
51a	Social security (FICA) tax on tip income not reported to employer *(attach Form 4137)*	51a	
51b	Uncollected employee FICA and RRTA tax on tips *(from Form W-2)*	51b	
52	Tax on an IRA *(attach Form 5329)*	52	
53	Advance earned income credit (EIC) payments received *(from Form W-2)*	53	
54	**Total tax.** Add lines 47 through 53 ▶	54	

06

Payments Attach Forms W-2, W-2G, and W-2P to front.

55	Total Federal income tax withheld	55			
56	1981 estimated tax payments and amount applied from 1980 return	56			
57	Earned income credit. If line 32a is under $10,000, see page 15 of Instructions	57			
58	Amount paid with Form 4868	58			
59	Excess FICA and RRTA tax withheld (two or more employers)	59			
60	Credit for Federal tax on special fuels and oils *(attach Form 4136 or 4136–T)*	60			
61	Regulated Investment Company credit *(attach Form 2439)*	61			
62	**Total.** Add lines 55 through 61 ▶			62	

Refund or Balance Due

63	If line 62 is larger than line 54, enter amount **OVERPAID** ▶	63	
64	Amount of line 63 to be **REFUNDED TO YOU** ▶	64	
65	Amount of line 63 to be applied to your 1982 estimated tax ▶ 65		
66	If line 54 is larger than line 62, enter **BALANCE DUE**. Attach check or money order for full amount payable to "Internal Revenue Service." Write your social security number and "1981 Form 1040" on it ▶ (Check ▶ ☐ if Form 2210 (2210F) is attached. See page 16 of Instructions.) ▶ $	66	

Please Sign Here

Under penalties of perjury, I declare that I have examined this return, including accompanying schedules and statements, and to the best of my knowledge and belief, it is true, correct, and complete. Declaration of preparer (other than taxpayer) is based on all information of which preparer has any knowledge.

▶ Your signature Date ▶ Spouse's signature (if filing jointly, BOTH must sign even if only one had income)

Paid Preparer's Use Only

Preparer's signature ▶	Date	Check if self-employed ▶ ☐	Preparer's social security no.
Firm's name (or yours, if self-employed) and address ▶		E.I. No. ▶	
		ZIP code ▶	

some negatives and "less than" terms are used, as in items 19 and 31. Items 8b and 32b employ complex sentences, which should be avoided when designing for easy comprehension.

Configuration and Layout. Form 1040 and Form 1040A are easy to identify since each is color coded overall—pale blue for Form 1040 and pink for Form 1040A. A verbal description could further aid in identification, for example, "Long Form" for 1040, and "Short Form" for 1040A. Color coding is otherwise poorly applied. For example, color-coded dots could be used in the upper left-hand corner to facilitate identification of the overall form. The caution note in item 32b could be colored yellow; the refund item, green; the balance due, red; and so on.

Space or location coding is effectively employed to set apart groups of items, and large-size black letters make effective use of size coding. Shape and pictorial coding are not employed in the form.

Print. Black print on a pale-blue background provides only fair contrast. Black print on a white background would provide optimal contrast. The 8-point size print may be somewhat marginal for reading, especially by elderly respondents. The smaller print used to indicate name, address, penalty, etc., and the interest-income subnote would be largely unreadable by people with poor vision. The print has good stroke and character-width-to-height ratios and is unembellished. Upper- and lower-case printing is also aptly used.

Organization. Logical organization of Form 1040 could be improved if "exemptions" followed the income section. On the tax side, "credits" should logically follow the "other tax" section. Numbering sequences are somewhat confusing where subitems do not seem to follow logically, for example, 51a and 51b following item 50. Space does not appear to be optimally employed in some instances, where the privacy and paperwork acts are cited, seemingly to no purpose.

Fill-in. Spaces seem generally adequate for fill-in requirements except for "occupation" fill-in space. Subitems 3, 4, and 5 under item 6d provide excessive space, while subitem 2 is crowded. Fill-in aids are generally good, including the label printout to be attached from the mailed forms. Specific marks to be made in boxes are not clarified, while boxes and fill-in spaces are inconsistently located; thus the right-handed population, 90 percent of the total, block the legends on all boxes to the left of items with the writing hand. Boxes should be relocated for items 1 through 6, 35, and 36. The requirement for turning to the front of the sheet for items 32a and 33 also increases fill-in time.

Form 1040A

Form 1040A is essentially a short version of Form 1040 (see exhibit D). The overall color is pink, which detracts from the reading-contrast effectiveness. Instead, a pink dot could be used for color coding the form. A word label, "Short Form," would also help in identifying the form.

Content. The caution note on page 2 contains a technical term, *nominee,* which should be simplified. The note also contains complex sentences with conjunctions. These could be improved to enhance readability.

Configuration. The caution note on page 2 could be color coded yellow, while other sections could also be appropriately color coded, as explained in the critique of Form 1040.

Print. Print size for name and address, items 5d (1) through (5), and the penalty clause, may be difficult for some elderly to read.

EXHIBIT D
U.S. Form 1040A, 1981, Income Tax Summary

Form **1040A** Department of the Treasury—Internal Revenue Service
U.S. Individual Income Tax Return **1981** (B) OMB No. 1545-0085

Use IRS label. Otherwise, please print or type.

Your first name and initial (if joint return, also give spouse's name and initial) | Last name | Your social security number
Present home address (Number and street, including apartment number, or rural route) | Spouse's social security no.
City, town or post office, State and ZIP code | Your occupation ▶ | Spouse's occupation ▶

Presidential Election Campaign ▶ Do you want $1 to go to this fund? . . . Yes | No
If joint return, does your spouse want $1 to go to this fund? . . . Yes | No
Note: Checking "Yes" will not increase your tax or reduce your refund.

For Privacy Act and Paperwork Reduction Act Notice, see page 23 of Instructions

Filing Status Check Only One Box.
1 ☐ Single
2 ☐ Married filing joint return (even if only one had income)
3 ☐ Married filing separate return. Enter spouse's social security no. above and full name here ▶
4 ☐ Head of household (with qualifying person). (See page 8 of Instructions.) If he or she is your unmarried child, enter child's name ▶

Exemptions Always check the box labeled Yourself. Check other boxes if they apply.
5a ☐ Yourself ☐ 65 or over ☐ Blind
b ☐ Spouse ☐ 65 or over ☐ Blind
Enter number of boxes checked on 5a and b ▶ ☐
c First names of your dependent children who lived with you ▶
Enter number of children listed on 5c ▶ ☐

d Other dependents:

(1) Name	(2) Relationship	(3) Number of months lived in your home.	(4) Did dependent have income of $1,000 or more?	(5) Did you provide more than one-half of dependent's support?

Enter number of other dependents ▶ ☐
Add numbers entered in boxes above ▶ ☐

6 Total number of exemptions claimed . . .

Please Attach Copy B of Forms W-2 Here

7 Wages, salaries, tips, etc. (Attach Forms W-2. See page 10 of Instructions) . . . 7
8a Interest income . . (Complete page 2 if over $400 or you have any All-Savers interest) . . . 8a
b Dividends . . . (Complete page 2 if over $400) . . . 8b
c Total (add lines 8a and 8b) . . . 8c
d Exclusion (See page 11 of Instructions) . . . 8d
e Subtract line 8d from line 8c (but not less than zero) . . . 8e
9a Unemployment compensation (insurance). Total received from Form(s) 1099–UC
b Taxable amount, if any, from worksheet on page 12 of Instructions . . . 9b
10 Adjusted gross income (add lines 7, 8e, and 9b). If under $10,000, see page 13 of Instructions on "Earned Income Credit" . . . 10
11 Multiply $1,000 by the total number of exemptions claimed on line 6 . . . 11
12 Taxable income (subtract line 11 from line 10) . . . 12
13a Credit for contributions to candidates for public office. (See page 13 of Instructions) . . . 13a

IF YOU WANT IRS TO FIGURE YOUR TAX, PLEASE STOP HERE AND SIGN BELOW.

Attach Payment Here

b Total Federal income tax withheld (If line 7 is more than $29,700, see page 13 of Instructions) . . . 13b
c Earned income credit (from page 14 of Instructions) . . . 13c
14 Total (add lines 13a, b, and c) . . . 14
15a Tax on the amount on line 12. (See page 15 of Instructions; then find your tax in the Tax Table on pages 17–22) . . . 15a
b Advance earned income credit (EIC) (from Form W-2) . . . 15b
16 Total (add lines 15a and 15b) . . . 16
17 If line 14 is larger than line 16, enter amount to be REFUNDED TO YOU . . . ▶ 17
18 If line 16 is larger than line 14, enter BALANCE DUE. Attach check or money order for full amount payable to "Internal Revenue Service." Write your social security number and "1981 Form 1040A" on it. ▶ 18

Please Sign Here
Under penalties of perjury, I declare that I have examined this return, including accompanying schedules and statements, and to the best of my knowledge and belief, it is true, correct, and complete. Declaration of preparer (other than taxpayer) is based on all information of which preparer has any knowledge.
▶ Your signature | Date | ▶ Spouse's signature (If filing jointly, BOTH must sign even if only one had income)

Paid Preparer's Use Only
Preparer's signature ▶ | Date | Check if self-employed ▶ ☐ | Preparer's social security no.
Firm's name (or yours, if self-employed) and address ▶ | E.I. No. ▶ | ZIP code ▶

Form **1040A** (1981)

EXHIBIT D (continued)
U.S. Form 1040A, 1981, reverse side

CAUTION: You may **NOT** file Form 1040A (you must file Form 1040 instead) if any of the following apply to you:

- You could be claimed as a dependent on your parents' return AND had interest, dividends, or other unearned income of $1,000 or more.
- You had a foreign financial account or were a grantor of, or transferor to, a foreign trust.
- You received interest or dividends as a nominee (in your name) for someone else.
- You received or paid accrued interest on securities transferred between interest payment dates.
- You received any capital gain distributions.

Note: *You may also be required to file Form 1040 for other reasons. See pages 4 and 5 of Instructions.*

Part I Interest Income

If you received more than $400 in interest or you received any interest from All-Savers Certificates, you must complete Part I and list the names of the payers and the amounts of the interest on the lines below. See page 10 of the Instructions for what interest to report.

Name of payer	Amount	
1a Interest income (other than qualifying interest from All-Savers Certificates).		
1b Total. Add above amounts		
1c Qualifying interest from All-Savers Certificates. (List payers and amounts even if $400 or less.) See page 11 of Instructions.		
1d Total		
1e Exclusion (See page 11 of Instructions)		
1f Subtract line 1e from line 1d. **Caution:** *No part of the amount on line 1f may be excluded on Form 1040A, line 8d*		
2 **Total interest income (add lines 1b and 1f).** Enter here and on Form 1040A, line 8a		

Part II Dividend Income

If you received more than $400 in ordinary dividends and nontaxable distributions, list the names of the payers and the amounts of the dividends on the lines below. Be sure to include any nontaxable distributions on these lines. They will be deducted on line 5 below. See page 10 of the Instructions for a definition of ordinary dividends and nontaxable distributions.

Name of payer	Amount	
3		
4 Total. Add above amounts		
5 Nontaxable distributions (See Instructions for adjustment to basis)		
6 **Total dividend income (subtract line 5 from line 4).** Enter here and on Form 1040A, line 8b		

☆ U.S. GOVERNMENT PRINTING OFFICE: 1981—0-343-265 E.I.#13-2687299

Organization. The logical sequence is generally effective, although item 13b relating to item 7 seems to be out of sequence. Space appears to be somewhat overused, where item 7 and the sideways instructions both indicate that the W-2 Form should be attached. Sideway instructions could be arranged in the horizontal position to improve readability.

Fill-in. Fill-in boxes are inconsistently located with respect to item listing (refer to comments made in the critique of Form 1040).

Form 1040, Schedules A and B

This form is used to itemize interest and dividend income and to list detailed deductions (see exhibit E). The black on white design provides excellent reading contrast. A color-coded blue dot could be included in the upper left-hand corner to identify its association with Form 1040. The inclusion of the small print identifying the "Department of Treasury" is of questionable value.

Content. The active imperative voice could be employed more effectively. (Note item 1 under "Medical and Dental Expenses.") Negative word usage in item 1 could be improved, for example, "Enter one-half of medical-care insurance premiums up to a maximum of $150."

The complex sentences of Parts I, II, and III of Schedule B could be simplified by reducing conjunctions and verbs. The technical term "nominee" should also be simplified.

Configuration. Better use could be made of coding techniques. For example, caution notes could be black on bright yellow background to highlight an area of special concern. Good configurational effects appear to operate with white on the black heading strips.

Print. Size of print seems generally good.

Organization. The order of items presented is generally logical, with side A covering deductions, side B, income. On Form 1040, however, Schedule B totals are entered before Schedule A totals. For proper sequencing, the sides should be reversed, that is, side A, interest and dividends, should be entered at items 8a and 8b, while the B side, deductions, should be entered at item 32b.

Fill-in. Spaces generally appear to be adequate for fill-in requirements. Name and social security number entries on both sides would seem to be redundant.

Form 1040, Schedule E, Supplemental Income

This form provides for summarizing profits or losses from property and business enterprises (see exhibit F). It is included in the Form 1040 packet.

Content. Several terms may be unfamiliar to some respondents, for example, "royalties," "estate or trusts," or "windfall profit." Complex sentences are employed, which detract from readability, such as in Part II, the risk-explanation items.

Configuration and Layout. Coding methods could be employed to enhance recognition, for example, a color-coded dot at the upper left-hand corner to identify Schedule E with Form 1040. Pictorial coding could also be used to enhance readability, such as a small building silhouette to denote property.

Print. The black print on a white background provides for the best contrast. The small-print-heading columns under the partnership and depreciation sections are difficult to read, which might be a problem for elderly respondents.

EXHIBIT E
U.S. Form 1040, Schedules A & B, Itemized Deductions

Schedules A&B (Form 1040)
Department of the Treasury Internal Revenue Service (B)

Schedule A—Itemized Deductions

(Schedule B is on back)

▶ Attach to Form 1040. ▶ See Instructions for Schedules A and B (Form 1040).

OMB No. 1545-0074
1981
07

Name(s) as shown on Form 1040 | Your social security number

Medical and Dental Expenses (Do not include expenses reimbursed or paid by others.) *(See page 17 of Instructions.)*

1 One-half (but not more than $150) of insurance premiums you paid for medical care. (Be sure to include in line 10 below.) . ▶
2 Medicine and drugs .
3 Enter 1% of Form 1040, line 31 . . .
4 Subtract line 3 from line 2. If line 3 is more than line 2, enter zero . . . . .
5 Balance of insurance premiums for medical care not entered on line 1 . . . .
6 Other medical and dental expenses:
a Doctors, dentists, nurses, etc. . . .
b Hospitals . . . .
c Transportation . . . .
d Other (itemize—include hearing aids, dentures, eyeglasses, etc.) ▶
7 Total (add lines 4 through 6d) . . . .
8 Enter 3% of Form 1040, line 31 . . .
9 Subtract line 8 from line 7. If line 8 is more than line 7, enter zero . . . . .
10 Total medical and dental expenses (add lines 1 and 9). Enter here and on line 33 . ▶

Taxes *(See page 18 of Instructions.)*

11 State and local income . . . . . .
12 Real estate . . . .
13 a General sales (see sales tax tables) .
b General sales on motor vehicles . .
14 Personal property . . . .
15 Other (itemize) ▶
16 Total taxes (add lines 11 through 15). Enter here and on line 34 . . . . ▶

Interest Expense *(See page 18 of Instructions.)*

17 Home mortgage . . . .
18 Credit and charge cards . . . . . .
19 Other (itemize) ▶
20 Total interest expense (add lines 17 through 19). Enter here and on line 35 ▶

Contributions *(See page 19 of Instructions.)*

21 a Cash contributions (If you gave $3,000 or more to any one organization, report those contributions on line 21b) .
b Cash contributions totaling $3,000 or more to any one organization (show to whom you gave and how much you gave) ▶
22 Other than cash (see page 19 of Instructions for required statement) . . . .
23 Carryover from prior years . . . . .
24 Total contributions (add lines 21a through 23). Enter here and on line 36 ▶

Casualty or Theft Loss(es) *(You must attach Form 4684 if line 29 is $1,000 or more, OR if certain other situations apply.) (See page 19 of Instructions.)*

25 Loss before reimbursement . . . .
26 Insurance or other reimbursement you received or expect to receive . . . .
27 Subtract line 26 from line 25. If line 26 is more than line 25, enter zero . . .
28 Enter $100 or amount from line 27, whichever is smaller . . . .
29 Total casualty or theft loss(es) (subtract line 28 from line 27). Enter here and on line 37 ▶

Miscellaneous Deductions *(See page 19 of Instructions.)*

30 a Union dues . . . .
b Tax return preparation fee . . . .
31 Other (itemize) ▶
32 Total miscellaneous deductions (add lines 30a through 31). Enter here and on line 38 . . . . ▶

Summary of Itemized Deductions **A**
(See page 20 of Instructions.)

33 Total medical and dental—from line 10 .
34 Total taxes—from line 16 . . . . .
35 Total interest—from line 20 . . . .
36 Total contributions—from line 24 . . .
37 Total casualty or theft loss(es)—from line 29 .
38 Total miscellaneous—from line 32 . .
39 Add lines 33 through 38 . . . . .
40 If you checked Form 1040, Filing Status box:
2 or 5, enter $3,400 . . . .
1 or 4, enter $2,300 . . . .
3, enter $1,700 . . . . .
41 Subtract line 40 from line 39. Enter here and on Form 1040, line 32b. (If line 40 is more than line 39, see the Instructions for line 41 on page 20.) . . . . . ▶

For Paperwork Reduction Act Notice, see Form 1040 Instructions.

Schedules A&B (Form 1040) 1981 **Schedule B—Interest and Dividend Income** OMB No. 1545–0074 Page **2**

Name(s) as shown on Form 1040 (Do not enter name and social security number if shown on other side) | **Your social security number**

Part I Interest Income

If you received more than $400 in interest or you received any interest from an All-Savers Certificate, you must complete Part I and list ALL interest received. Also complete Part III if you received more than $400 in interest. See page 8 of the Instructions to find out what interest to report. Then answer the questions in Part III, below. If you received interest as a nominee for another, or you received or paid accrued interest on securities transferred between interest payment dates, please see page 20 of the Instructions.

Name of payer	Amount
1a Interest income (other than qualifying interest from All-Savers Certificates).	
1b Total. Add above amounts	
1c Qualifying interest from All-Savers Certificates. (List payers and amounts even if $400 or less.) See page 20 of Instructions.	
1d Total	
1e Exclusion (See page 20 of Instructions) .	
1f Subtract line 1e from line 1d. **Caution:** *No part of the amount on line 1f may be excluded on Form 1040, line 8d*.	
2 Total interest income (add lines 1b and 1f). Enter here and on Form 1040, line 8a	

Part II Dividend Income

If you received more than $400 in gross dividends (including capital gain distributions) and other distributions on stock, complete Part II and Part III. Please see page 9 of the Instructions. Then answer the questions in Part III, below. If you received dividends as a nominee for another, please see page 21 of the Instructions.

Name of payer	Amount
3	
4 Total. Add above amounts	
5 Capital gain distributions. Enter here and on line 13, Schedule D. See Note below . . .	
6 Nontaxable distributions (See Instructions for adjustment to basis)	
7 Total (add lines 5 and 6)	
8 Total dividend income (subtract line 7 from line 4). Enter here and on Form 1040, line 8b	

B

Note: *If you received capital gain distributions for the year and you do not need Schedule D to report any other gains or losses or to compute the alternative tax, do not file that schedule. Instead, enter 40% of your capital gain distributions on Form 1040, line 13.*

Part III Foreign Accounts and Foreign Trusts

If you received more than $400 of interest or dividends, OR if you had a foreign account or were a grantor of, or a transferor to, a foreign trust, you must answer both questions in Part III. Please see page 21 of the Instructions.

	Yes	No
9 At any time during the tax year, did you have an interest in or a signature or other authority over a bank account, securities account, or other financial account in a foreign country?		
10 Were you the grantor of, or transferor to, a foreign trust which existed during the current tax year, whether or not you have any beneficial interest in it? . . . . If "Yes," you may have to file Forms 3520, 3520–A, or 926.		

For Paperwork Reduction Act Notice, see Form 1040 Instructions. 23-188-5979

☆U.S. GOVERNMENT PRINTING OFFICE: 1981—343-254

EXHIBIT F

U.S. Form 1040, Schedule E, Supplemental Income Schedule

SCHEDULE E (Form 1040)
Department of the Treasury Internal Revenue Service (B)

Supplemental Income Schedule

(From rents and royalties, partnerships, estates and trusts, etc.)
▶ Attach to Form 1040. ▶ See Instructions for Schedule E (Form 1040).

OMB No. 1545–0074

1981
15

Name(s) as shown on Form 1040 | Your social security number

Part I Rent and Royalty Income or Loss.

1 Are any of the expenses listed below for a vacation home or similar dwelling rented to others (see Instructions)? . ☐ Yes ☐ No

2 If you checked "Yes" to question 1, did you or a member of your family occupy the vacation home or similar dwelling for more than 14 days during the tax year? . . . . ☐ Yes ☐ No

Rental and Royalty Income (describe property in Part V)		Properties A	Properties B	Properties C		Totals
3 a Rents received					3	
b Royalties received						
Rental and Royalty Expenses						
4 Advertising	4					
5 Auto and travel	5					
6 Cleaning and maintenance	6					
7 Commissions	7					
8 Insurance	8					
9 Interest	9					
10 Legal and other professional fees . .	10					
11 Repairs	11					
12 Supplies	12					
13 Taxes (do NOT include Windfall Profit Tax, see Part III, line 35)	13					
14 Utilities	14					
15 Wages and salaries	15					
16 Other (list) ▶						
17 Total deductions (add lines 4 through 16)	17				17	
18 Depreciation expense (see Instructions), or Depletion (attach computation)	18				18	
19 Total (add lines 17 and 18)	19					
20 Income or (loss) from rental or royalty properties (subtract line 19 from line 3a (rents) or 3b (royalties))	20					

21 Add properties with profits on line 20, and enter total profits here 21

22 Add properties with losses on line 20, and enter total (losses) here . . . . 22 ( )

23 Combine amounts on lines 21 and 22, and enter net profit or (loss) here 23

24 Net farm rental profit or (loss) from Form 4835, line 50 24

25 Total rental or royalty income or (loss). Combine amounts on lines 23 and 24. Enter here and include in line 37 on page 2 25

For Paperwork Reduction Act Notice, see Form 1040 Instructions.

E

EXHIBIT F (continued)
Schedule E, reverse side

Schedule E (Form 1040) 1981 Page 2

Part II Income or Losses from Partnerships, Estates or Trusts, or Small Business Corporations

If you report a loss below, do you have amounts invested in that activity for which you are not "at risk" (see Instructions)? ☐ Yes ☐ No
If "Yes," and your loss exceeded your amount "at risk," did you limit your loss to your amount "at risk"? . . . . . . ☐ Yes ☐ No

	(a) Name	(b) Employer identification number	(c) Net loss (see Instructions for "at risk" limitations)	(d) Net income
Partnerships				
	26 Add amounts in columns (c) and (d) and enter here 26		( )	
	27 Combine amounts in columns (c) and (d), line 26, and enter net income or (loss) 27			
	28 Additional first-year depreciation from 1980/1981 fiscal-year partnerships. Enter amount from Form 1065, Schedule K–1, line 2, but not more than $2,000 ($4,000 if a joint return) . . . 28			( )
	29 Total partnership income or (loss). Combine lines 27 and 28. Enter here and include in line 37 . 29			
Estates or Trusts				
	30 Add amounts in columns (c) and (d) and enter here 30		( )	
	31 Total estate or trust income or (loss). Combine amounts in columns (c) and (d), line 30. Enter here and include in line 37 31			
Small Business Corporations				
	32 Add amounts in columns (c) and (d) and enter here 32		( )	
	33 Total small business corporation income or (loss). Combine amounts in columns (c) and (d), line 32. Enter here and include in line 37 33			

Part III Windfall Profit Tax Summary

34 Windfall Profit Tax Credit or Refund received in 1981 (see Instructions)	34	
35 Windfall Profit Tax withheld in 1981 (see Instructions)	35	( )
36 Combine amounts on lines 34 and 35. Enter here and include in line 37	36	

Part IV Summary

37 TOTAL income or (loss). Combine lines 25, 29, 31, 33, and 36. Enter here and on Form 1040, line 17 . ▶	37	
38 Farmers and fishermen: Enter your share of gross farming and fishing income applicable to Parts I and II 38		

Part V Depreciation Claimed in Part I.—Complete only if property was placed in service before January 1, 1981. For more space, use Form 4562. If you placed any property in service after December 31, 1980, use Form 4562 for all property; do NOT complete Part V.

	(a) Description and location of property	(b) Date acquired	(c) Cost or other basis	(d) Depreciation allowed or allowable in prior years	(e) Depreciation method	(f) Life or rate	(g) Depreciation for this year
Property A							
	Totals (Property A)			. . . .			
Property B							
	Totals (Property B)			. . . .			
Property C							
	Totals (Property C)			. . . .			

☆ U.S. GOVERNMENT PRINTING OFFICE: 1981—O-343-259 58-040-1110 343–062–1

Organization. The logical order of categories could be improved by grouping all property items together, then the business items. Rent and royalty could be grouped with estates or trusts and property depreciation; partnerships could be grouped with small business corporations, farmers and fishermen, and windfall profits.

The headings used for partnerships—Name, Employer I.D., and the like—are confusing in that they are also used to head columns for estates or trusts and small business corporations. The form also presents a cluttered effect where items are numbered both at the left and right of the item.

Fill-in. Crowding of information is likely in part V, particularly under (c), "Depreciation method." Also, in parts I and II, fill-in boxes for yes-no responses are located to the left of the words. Printing of the sectional headings is also located perpendicular to the normal reading angle on page 2.

Form 1040, Schedules R and RP, Credit for the Elderly

This form is heavily loaded with words and explanations (see exhibit G). It has good black-on-white contrast, with print 8 and 10 point size. However, the generally poorer vision of an elderly population would indicate the need for larger print.

Content. Many of the items contain single sentences with double and triple conditions, such as "one 65 or over, and one under 65 with income from a public retirement system." Such sentence structure tends to elicit errors in interpretation and fill-in.

"Less than" items are also poorly structured for comprehension, for example, items 3 and 7 on Schedule R, and 4, 6, and 10 on Schedule RP. Multiple conjunctions and verbs are employed in single sentences, as "If you received nontaxable pensions (social security, etc.) of $3,750, or your adjusted gross income (Form 1040, line 32a) was $17,500 or more, you cannot take credit for the elderly." The term "annuity" may also be difficult to understand for some respondents.

Configuration. Headings that highlight conditions for use of the schedules would be helpful, such as "Use this form for public (versus nonpublic) retirement systems." Color coding could also be employed to reduce form-recognition time, for example, a blue dot for public retirement systems and a yellow dot for nonpublic. Other modes of coding could also be effectively applied to facilitate recognition of subheading and item groups, for instance, earned-income items could be spatially coded or grouped to be distinct from pension income.

Print. A larger size print—at least 10 point—generally appears to be needed for elderly respondents. The printing in these schedules is otherwise well designed.

Organization. Logical sequencing could be improved. A multiplicity of distinctions about age and income must be sorted out or gleaned from an awkward sentence structure. The sentences are too long and wordy. Sequencing of the groups, however, generally is adequate.

Space saving could be effected by reducing sentence length and by eliminating unnecessary information. For example, citation of the Paperwork Act and detailed form identification, such as OMB numbers, do not seem to be pertinent.

Fill-in. Excessive depth of fill-in space is used for entering dollar amounts. This is largely due to the structure of adjacent explanatory paragraphs. Fill-in boxes for filing status should be located to the right of descriptive text to prevent the hand from covering the items to be filled in.

Schedules R & RP (Form 1040)
Department of the Treasury Internal Revenue Service (B)

Credit for the Elderly

▶ See Instructions for Schedules R and RP.
▶ Attach to Form 1040. ▶ Schedule RP is on back.

OMB No. 1545-0074
1981
21

Name(s) as shown on Form 1040 | Your social security number

Please Note: *IRS will figure your Credit for the Elderly and compute your tax. Please see "IRS Will Figure Your Tax and Some of Your Credits" on page 3 of the Form 1040 instructions and complete the applicable lines on Form 1040 and Schedule R or RP.*

Should You Use Schedule R or RP?

If you are:	And were:	Use Schedule:
Single	▶ 65 or over	R
	▶ under 65 and had income from a public retirement system	RP
Married, filing separate return [1]	▶ 65 or over (unless joining in the election to use Schedule RP with your spouse who is under 65 and had income from a public retirement system)	R
	▶ under 65 and had income from a public retirement system (unless your spouse is 65 or over and does not join in the election to use Schedule RP)	RP
Married, filing joint return	▶ both 65 or over	R
	▶ one 65 or over, and one under 65 with no income or income other than from a public retirement system	R
	▶ both under 65 and one or both had income from a public retirement system	RP
	▶ one 65 or over, and one under 65 with income from a public retirement system	R or RP [2]

[1] You can take the credit on a separate return ONLY if you and your spouse lived apart for the whole year. See "Purpose" in Schedules R&RP instructions for limitation.
[2] Figure your credit on both schedules to see which gives you more credit.

Schedule R **Credit for the Elderly—For People 65 or Over**
If you received nontaxable pensions (social security, etc.) of $3,750 or more or your adjusted gross income (Form 1040, line 32a) was $17,500 or more, you cannot take the credit for the elderly. Do not file this schedule.

Filing Status and Age (check only one box)
- A ☐ Single, 65 or over
- B ☐ Married filing joint return, only one spouse 65 or over
- C ☐ Married filing joint return, both 65 or over
- D ☐ Married filing separate return, 65 or over, and did not live with spouse at any time in 1981

R

1 Enter: { $2,500 if you checked box A or B; $3,750 if you checked box C; $1,875 if you checked box D } . . . **1**

2 a Enter amounts you received as pensions or annuities under the Social Security Act or under the Railroad Retirement Acts (but not supplemental annuities), and certain other exclusions from gross income (see instructions). **If none, enter zero** . . . **2a**

b Enter amount from Form 1040, line 32a . . **2b**

c Enter: { $7,500 if you checked box A; $10,000 if you checked box B or C; $5,000 if you checked box D } . **2c**

d Subtract line 2c from 2b. If line 2c is more than line 2b, enter zero . . . **2d**

e Enter one-half (½) of line 2d . . . **2e**

3 Add lines 2a and 2e. (If line 3 is the same or more than line 1, you cannot take the credit; do not file this schedule. If line 3 is less than line 1, go on to line 4.) . . . **3**

4 Subtract line 3 from line 1 . . . **4**

5 Multiply line 4 by 15% (.15) . . . **5**

6 Enter amount of tax from Form 1040, line 37. (If this amount is zero, you cannot take the credit; do not file this schedule.) . . . **6**

7 Enter the amount from line 5 or line 6, above, whichever is less. This is your **Credit for the Elderly.** Enter the same amount on Form 1040, line 39 . . . ▶ **7**

For Paperwork Reduction Act Notice, see Form 1040 Instructions.

Schedules R&RP (Form 1040) 1981 — OMB No. 1545-0074

Name(s) as shown on Form 1040 | Your social security number

Schedule RP **Credit for the Elderly—For People Under 65 Who Had Pension or Annuity Income from a Public Retirement System** 21

If you are under 72 and received nontaxable pensions (social security, etc.) of $2,500 or more or your earned income (salaries, wages, etc.) was $3,950 or more, you cannot take the credit for the elderly. Do not file this schedule.

Name(s) of public retirement system(s)

Filing Status and Age (check only one box)

- A ☐ Single, under 65
- B ☐ Married filing joint return, one spouse is under 65, and that person had income from a public retirement system. (If you checked this box and had community property income, see Community Property Income on page 26 of the instructions.)
- C ☐ Married filing joint return, both under 65. (If you checked this box and had community property income, see Community Property Income on page 26 of the instructions.)
- D ☐ Married filing separate return, under 65, and did not live with your spouse at any time in 1981.
- E ☐ Married filing separate return, 65 or over, did not live with your spouse at any time in 1981, and you are joining with your spouse in electing to use Schedule RP.

RP

Column (b)—Fill out column (b) whether you file a separate or joint return.
Column (a)—Fill out column (a) if you file a joint return. Use it only to show amounts for:
- **The wife, if both of you were under 65, or**
- **The spouse who was 65 or over.**

	Line	(a)	(b)
1 Enter: $2,500 if you checked box A; $3,750 if you checked box B or C. Allocate this amount between you and your spouse, but do not enter more than $2,500 for either of you. It will generally be to your benefit to allocate the greater amount to the spouse with more retirement income; $1,875 if you checked box D or box E	1		
2 Enter: **a** Amounts you received as pensions or annuities under the Social Security Act or under the Railroad Retirement Acts (but not supplemental annuities), and certain other exclusions from gross income (see instructions). **If none, enter zero**	2a		
b Earned income such as wages, salaries, fees, etc. you received (does not apply to people 72 or over). (See page 26 of instructions for definition of earned income.): (i) If you are under 62, enter earned income that is over $900	2b(i)		
(ii) If you are 62 or over but under 72, enter an amount that you will figure as follows: If earned income is $1,200 or less, enter zero; If earned income is over $1,200 but not over $1,700, enter one-half of the amount over $1,200; If earned income is over $1,700, enter the amount over $1,450	2b(ii)		
3 Add lines 2a and 2b	3		
4 Subtract line 3 from line 1. (If the result for either column is more than zero, go on. If the result for either column is zero or less, do not complete the rest of the lines in that column. If the result for both columns is zero or less, you cannot take the credit; do not file this schedule.)	4		
5 Retirement income: **a If under 65—** Enter only income from pensions and annuities under public retirement systems (e.g. Federal, State Governments, etc.) that you received as a result of your services or services of your spouse that you reported as income. Do not enter social security, railroad retirement or certain other payments reported on line 2a	5a		
b If 65 or over— Enter total of pensions and annuities, interest, dividends, proceeds of retirement bonds, and amounts you received from individual retirement arrangements and individual retirement annuities that you reported as income, and gross rents from: Schedule E, Part I, columns A–C, line 3a. Also include your share of gross rents from partnerships and your share of taxable rents from estates and trusts	5b		
6 Enter amount from line 4 or line 5, whichever is less	6		
7 Add amounts in columns (a) and (b) of line 6. Enter total here ▶	7		
8 Multiply line 7 by 15% (.15)	8		
9 Enter amount of tax from Form 1040, line 37. (If this amount is zero, you cannot take the credit; do not file this schedule.)	9		
10 Enter the amount from line 8 or line 9, above, whichever is less. This is your **Credit for the Elderly.** Enter the same amount on Form 1040, line 39 ▶	10		

For Paperwork Reduction Act Notice, see Form 1040 Instructions. ☆ U.S. GOVERNMENT PRINTING OFFICE: 1981 -343-262 (31-0598032)

IRS Forms Evaluation

The Internal Revenue Service, a bureaucracy, is politically sensitive to outside pressure due to its citizen contacts and revenue-collection functions. The IRS itself has estimated that over 300 million man-hours are expended annually by the citizenry in filling out tax forms. Improvements in forms efficiency from the respondent's standpoint is an acknowledged if not immediate design goal of the IRS. Pressures on the IRS from Congress for form changes to cover new tax provisions receive the highest priority. Each November the new form goes to press, often without a great deal of functional review or input from respondents. In fact, the IRS does not test for reading comprehension or readability using representative respondent population samples. Rather, the agency tends to rely on readability consulting specialists for forms-design advice and evaluation.

On occasion, the IRS undertakes pilot studies to obtain reaction to new forms. A short form, 1040S, was recently sent to 30,000 taxpayers in Georgia. In this new form, red type is used in the margin to guide the taxpayer from Step 1 through Step 9 (where the form is signed). Design includes substituting the term "deduction" for "exemption," with other modifications such as the use of plus and minus signs to simplify computation instructions. Evaluation and development of the form design will continue for two or three years, after which the form will be introduced throughout the country (*Moneysworth*, 1982).

U.S. Postal Service (PS) Forms

Two PS forms, also used extensively, are illustrated in exhibits H and I. PS Form 3575, Change of Address Order, is filled out by the general public to notify a local post office of a new address. Word content could be reduced. For example, the first statement on the left side might read, "First class mail and parcels of value will be forwarded for a maximum of one year." A form title is lacking on the fill-in side of

EXHIBIT H

U.S. Postal Service Form 3575, Change of Address Order

THIS ORDER PROVIDES for the forwarding of First-Class Mail and all parcels of obvious value for a period not to exceed 1 year.	**Print or Type** *(Last Name, First Name, Middle Initial)*
CHANGE OF ADDRESS IS FOR: ☐ **Entire Family** *(When last name of family members differ, separate orders for each last name must be filed.)* ☐ **Individual Signer Only**	OLD ADDRESS — **No. and St., Apt., Suite, P.O. Box or R.D. No. (In care of)**
	OLD ADDRESS — City, State, and ZIP Code
I agree to pay forwarding postage for newspapers and magazines for 90 days. ☐ NO ☐ YES	NEW ADDRESS — **No. and St., Apt., Suite, P.O. Box or R.D. No. (In care of)**
USPS USE ONLY Clerk/Carrier Endorsement	NEW ADDRESS — City, State, and ZIP Code
Carrier Route Number	**Effective Date** | **If Temporary, Expiration Date**
Date Entered	**Sign Here** ▶ | **Date Signed**

PS Form 3575, Sep. 1981 — *Signature & title of person authorizing address change. (DO NOT print or type.)*

☆ U.S. GOVERNMENT PRINTING OFFICE: 1982-554-871

EXHIBIT I

U.S. Postal Service Form 3573, Change of Address Notice to Correspondence

PS Form 3576
May 1978

As soon as you know your new address, mail this card to all the people, businesses, and publishers who send you mail.

For publishers, paste old label over name and old address sections and complete new address section.

Your Name	Print or Type–Last Name, First Name, Middle Initial	New Area Code and Telephone No. if known
Old Address	No. and Street, Apt., Suite, P.O. Box or R.D. No.	
	City, State and ZIP Code	
New Address	No. and Street, Apt., Suite, P.O. Box or R.D. No. (In care of)	
	City, State and ZIP Code	
Sign Here		Date new address in effect
		Account No. (If any)

Receiver: Be sure to record the above new address in your address book at home or office.

the form. Color coding could improve recognition functions. For example, yellow could be used for the old address and green for the new.

The print should be much larger to accommodate elderly respondents with poor vision. The organization could be logically arranged proceeding from left to right: name, address changes, effective date, postage guarantees and conditions of change, and signature.

The fill-in spaces are adequate, with the printing properly located above or to the left for typewriter or manual completion. The fill-in boxes, however, should be to the right of descriptive wording.

The second form is PS Form 3573, Change of Address Notice to Correspondents. Respondents completing this form also cut across the entire demographic spectrum of the American public (see exhibit I). Here, as in Form 3575, a title is lacking on the completion side. The print is blue on a white background, where black on white is preferred to provide the best contrast. Color coding could be accomplished by using colored dots at the upper left.

Print size is 10 point for the bold headings, but the other print is too small for easy readability by an older population or others with poor vision. The organization is logically sound, with adequate fill-in spaces and acceptable layout.

STATE GOVERNMENT FORMS

New York State Form IT-201, Income Tax Return

The New York State income tax form (see exhibit J) requires that calculations completed for the federal Form 1040 be used in figuring the New York tax. The form incorporates both New York State and New York City personal income tax.

Content. The passive voice is employed on page 2 "Married persons filing separate NY returns on one form must also complete columns A and B. . . ." The active voice would be more effective in providing directions: "Married persons complete columns A and B when filing separate returns."

Negative words are used in Schedule C, while positive statements have been found to be more effective—"Use only for itemized deductions."

Configuration. The overall form is color-coded brown. Bold brown letters are employed to identify the form number, with headings and subheadings used to identify item content. However, coding has not been effectively used to simplify perception of form content. For example, the section on New York City tax, if presented in a different color than the rest of the form, would be clearly distinguished from state tax items.

Print. Dark brown print is used on a light brown background, which yields poor contrast. The main body of the form is set in 8 point type. Smaller print, aggravated by poor contrast, is virtually unreadable by the elderly population and others with weak vision, for example, item 25, "attach check or money order."

Organization. Sections are arranged as "Schedules" into logical groups. The form, however, is cluttered where reminders are used as fillers in unused space. Also, some sentences are more than 7 inches long, and headings are printed perpendicularly.

Fill-in. Fill-in spaces are generally adequate. Fill-in boxes, however, are inconsistently located to the left or right of the item. Vertical lines, such as those marking off digit groups for a Social Security number, have been found to interfere with fill-in responses.

New York State Form IT 201-ATT, Credits and Taxes

This form (exhibit K) supplements Form IT-201 in figuring additional credits and taxes.

EXHIBIT J

New York State & City of New York, Resident Income Tax Return, Form IT-201

Page 1

IT-201 New York State & City of New York Resident Income Tax Return 1981

Or Fiscal Year Ending 1982 R

PRINT OR TYPE

First name and initial (if joint or combined return, enter both names) Last name	Your social security number	Occupation(s)
Home address (number and street or rural route) Apt. No.	Spouse's social security number	School district name
City, village or post office State ZIP code	NY State county of residence	School district code

(A) FILING STATUS Check only ONE box

1. Single
2. Married filing joint return
3. Married filing separately on **one** return
4. Married filing separately on **separate** forms— (enter spouse's social security number above)
5. Qualifying widow(er) with dependent child or head of household

(B) CHANGE OF STATE RESIDENCE: if you were a New York State resident for only part of the year, enter the number of months of New York State residence and attach Schedule IT-360........ number of months

(C) CAN YOU BE CLAIMED as a dependent on another taxpayer's federal return?.............. YES NO

TAX COMPUTATION

			Column A	Column B
1	Total income *(from page 2, line 45)*	1		
2	New York adjustments *(from page 2, line 56)*	2		
3	Total New York income *(line 1 and add or subtract line 2)*	3		
4	NY deduction - **Check one** Standard *(see instructions page 9)* Itemized *(see page 2, line 67)* Enter amount	4		
5	Subtract line 4 from line 3	5		
6	Exemptions — Enter number claimed: Column A ___ x $750 =	6a		
	Column B ___ x $750 =	6b		
7	New York taxable income *(subtract line 6 from line 5 — if line 7 is over $17,000, see instructions for maximum tax on page 9)*	7		
8	State tax on line 7 amount *(from State Tax Rate Schedule)* OR Maximum tax *(from Form IT-250, line 14; fill in line 8a below)*	8		

			Column A	Column B
8a	Personal service taxable income *(from Form IT-250, line 12)*	8a		

CREDITS/OTHER TAXES

			Column A	Column B
9	Household credit *(see instructions page 10)*	9		
10	Subtract line 9 from line 8	10		
11	Other NY State credits *(from Form IT-201-ATT, line 9)*	11		
12	Subtract line 11 from line 10	12		
13	Other NY State taxes *(from Form IT-201-ATT, line 14)*	13		
14	Total New York State tax *(add lines 12 and 13)*	14		
15a	City of NY resident tax *(full-year City of NY residents only—from City Tax Rate Schedule)*	15a		
15b	Other City of NY tax *(from Form IT-201-ATT, line 20)*	15b		
16	Total NY State and City of NY taxes *(add lines 14, 15a and 15b)*	16		

PAYMENTS

			Column A	Column B
17	Real property tax credit *(from Form IT-214, line 13)* If any qualified member of household is 65 or older, check box.... Attach Form	17		
18	NY State tax withheld	18		
19	NY State estimated tax paid	19		
20	City of NY tax withheld	20		
21	City of NY estimated tax paid *(not City UBT)*	21		
22a	Total payments *(add lines 17 through 21)*	22a		

Reminders

- **Attach wage and tax statements.**
- **Sign your return.**

REFUND/DUE

			Column A	Column B
22b	Amount of payments applied to tax *(see instructions page 11)*	22b		
23	If line 22b is larger than line 16, enter amount **OVERPAID**	23		
24	Amount of line 23 to be **REFUNDED TO YOU**	24		
25	If line 16 is larger than line 22b, enter **BALANCE DUE** *(attach check or money order payable to NY State Income Tax)*	25		
26	Amount of line 23 to be applied to 1982 estimated tax — NY State	26		
27	City of NY	27		

For office use only

If you use a paid preparer and do **not** want NY tax forms mailed to you, check box

SIGN HERE

Your signature — Date — Your Telephone Number ( )

Spouse's signature (if filing jointly or separately on one return) — This entry is voluntary. See Instructions pg. 12.

Paid preparer's signature and address — Date

IT-201 (1981) **Remember to attach wage and tax statements** Page 2

Schedule A – Total Income

Complete the federal amount column entering these items as they appear on your federal return. Married persons filing separate NY returns on one form must also complete columns A and B to report their incomes as if separate federal returns were filed *(see instructions on page 13)*. If only the federal amount column is used, transfer the line 45 total to page 1, line 1, column A. If columns A and B are used, transfer only these line 45 totals to page 1, line 1.

		Federal Amount	Column A	Column B
28 Wages, salaries, tips, etc.	28			
29 Interest and dividend income *(after exclusion)*	29			
30 Refunds of state and local income taxes	30			
31 Alimony received	31			
32 Business income or (loss) *(attach copy of federal Schedule C, Form 1040)*	32			
33 Capital gain or (loss) *(attach copy of federal Schedule D, Form 1040)*	33			
34 40% of capital gain distributions not reported on line 33	34			
35 Supplemental gains or (losses) *(attach federal Form 4797)*	35			
36 Fully taxable pensions and annuities not reported on line 37	36			
37 Taxable amount of other pensions and annuities	37			
38 Rents and royalties — Enter the amounts from federal Schedule E, Form 1040 on lines 38 and 39 and attach a copy of Schedule E.	38			
39 Partnerships, estates and trusts and small business corporations	39			
40 Farm income or (loss) *(attach copy of federal Schedule F, Form 1040)*	40			
41 Taxable amount of unemployment compensation (insurance) *(see inst.)*	41			
42 Other income	42			
43 Total *(add lines 28 through 42)*	43			
44 Total adjustments to income *(federal)*	44			
45 **Total income** *(subtract line 44 from line 43; enter here and on pg. 1, line 1)*	45			

NOTE: If you are married and filing separate returns on one form and the total of A and B is not equal to the Federal Amount, attach an explanation.

Schedule B – New York Adjustments

Enter the amount of additions to and subtractions from your total income *(see instructions on page 14)*.

NY Additions:		Column A	Column B
46 Capital gain adjustments *(see instructions page 14)*	46		
47 Interest income on state and local bonds other than NY	47		
48 Other *(identify)* ______	48		
49 Total additions *(add lines 46, 47 and 48)*	49		

NY Subtractions:		Column A	Column B
50 State and local income tax refunds from line 30	50		
51 Tuition deduction *(from Form IT-270, line 9)*	51		
52 PASS fund deduction *(from Form IT-270, line 16)*	52		
53 Interest income on U.S. Govt. bonds	53		
54 Other *(identify)* ______	54		

		Column A	Column B
55 Total subtractions *(add lines 50 through 54)*	55	( )	( )
56 **New York adjustments** *(combine lines 49 and 55; enter the net additions or (subtractions) here and on page 1, line 2)*	56		

TAX RATE SCHEDULES are on the back cover of the instructions and on page 2 of Form IT-201-ATT.

FREE ASSISTANCE is available at any tax office listed on page 26 of instructions and on page 2 of Form IT-201-ATT.

MAIL YOUR RETURN TO:
New York State Income Tax
State Campus
Albany, New York 12227

Schedule C – NY Itemized Deduction

Enter on lines 57 through 63 the total of these items as they appear on federal Schedule A and make any required adjustments on lines 64 and 66 *(see instructions on page 17)*.
If you claim the standard deduction, do not use this schedule.

57 Total medical and dental expenses	57	
58 Total taxes	58	
59 Total interest expense	59	
60 Total contributions	60	
61 Total casualty or theft losses	61	
62 Total miscellaneous deductions	62	
63 Add lines 57 through 62	63	
64 Income taxes included in line 58	64	
65 Subtract line 64 from line 63	65	
66 Other adjustments *(see instructions on page 17)*	66	
67 **NY itemized deduction** *(line 65 and add or subtract line 66, enter here and on page 1, line 4)*	67	

(9/81) 13,000M (170)

EXHIBIT K
New York State, Summary of Other Credits and Taxes, Form IT-201 ATT

IT-201-ATT Summary of Other Credits and Taxes

Page 1

1981

Attachment to Form IT-201

New York State Department of Taxation and Finance

• Use only if any of these Other Credits or Taxes apply.

Name(s) as shown on Form IT-201	Your social security number

Schedule OC — Other NY State Credits *(see instructions page 18)*		Column A	Column B
1 Resident credit *(attach Form IT-112R and copy of other state(s) return)*	1		
2 Accumulation distribution credit *(attach computation)*	2		
3 State child and dependent care credit	3		
4 Catalytic agent credit	4		
5 Add lines 1 through 4	5		
6 Investment credit *(attach Form IT-212)*	6		
7 Mortgage recording tax credit	7		
8 Solar and wind energy credit *(attach Form IT-218)*	8		
9 Total *(add lines 5 through 8; enter here and on Form IT-201, page 1, line 11)*	9		

Schedule OT— Other NY State Taxes *(see instructions page 19)*		Column A	Column B
10a State separate tax on lump sum distributions *(attach Form IT-230 or IT-230.1)*	10a		
10b Resident credit against separate tax on lump sum distributions *(attach Form IT-112.1 and copy of other state(s) return)*	10b		
10c Subtract line 10b from 10a	10c		
11 State minimum income tax *(attach Form IT-220)*	11		
12 State separate tax on PASS funds *(attach Form IT-270)*	12		
13 Add-back of investment credit on early dispositions *(attach Form IT-212)*	13		
14 Total *(add lines 10c through 13, enter here and on Form IT-201, page 1, line 13)*	14		

Schedule NYC — Other City of NY Taxes *(see instructions page 19)*		Column A	Column B
15 City of NY nonresident earnings tax *(attach Form NYC-203)*	15		
16 Part-year City of NY resident tax *(attach Schedule IT-360)*	16		
17 City of NY minimum income tax *(attach Form IT-220)*	17		
18 City of NY separate tax on lump sum distributions *(attach Form IT-230 or IT-230.1)*	18		
19 City of NY separate tax on PASS funds *(attach Form IT-270)*	19		
20 Total *(add lines 15 through 19; enter here and on Form IT-201, page 1, line 15b)*	20		

New York State Tax Rate Schedule

If amount on Form IT-201, line 7 is:

over	but not over	Enter on Form IT-201, line 8:	
$ 0	$1,000		2% of amount on line 7
1,000	3,000	$20 plus	3% of amount over $1,000
3,000	5,000	80 plus	4% " " " 3,000
5,000	7,000	160 plus	5% " " " 5,000
7,000	9,000	260 plus	6% " " " 7,000
9,000	11,000	380 plus	7% " " " 9,000
11,000	13,000	520 plus	8% " " " 11,000
13,000	15,000	680 plus	9% " " " 13,000
15,000	17,000	860 plus	10% " " " 15,000
* 17,000	19,000	1,060 plus	11% " " " 17,000
19,000	21,000	1,280 plus	12% " " " 19,000
21,000	23,000	1,520 plus	13% " " " 21,000
23,000		1,780 plus	14% " " " 23,000

*** If the amount on Form IT-201, line 7 is more than $17,000, you may qualify for a New York State maximum tax rate of 10% on personal service income. See page 9 of the IT-201 instruction booklet and Form IT-250.**

City of New York Resident Tax Rate Schedule

If amount on Form IT-201, line 7 is:

over	but not over	Enter on Form IT-201, line 15a:	
$ 0	$1,000		0.9% of amount on line 7
1,000	3,000	$ 9 plus	1.4% of amount over $1,000
3,000	5,000	37 plus	1.8% " " " 3,000
5,000	7,000	73 plus	2.0% " " " 5,000
7,000	9,000	113 plus	2.3% " " " 7,000
9,000	11,000	159 plus	2.5% " " " 9,000
11,000	13,000	209 plus	2.7% " " " 11,000
13,000	15,000	263 plus	2.9% " " " 13,000
15,000	17,000	321 plus	3.1% " " " 15,000
17,000	19,000	383 plus	3.3% " " " 17,000
19,000	21,000	449 plus	3.5% " " " 19,000
21,000	23,000	519 plus	3.8% " " " 21,000
23,000	25,000	595 plus	4.0% " " " 23,000
25,000		675 plus	4.3% " " " 25,000

Telephone Assistance

For forms or publications, call toll free 1-800-462-8100.
For information, use only the number listed below for your area:

Albany (Capital District)	457-0111
Hauppauge	979-9896
Mineola	741-0950
New York City	488-3400
White Plains	948-3773
Elsewhere in New York State	1-800-342-3536

If you need to write instead of calling, please address your letter to:

New York State Department of
Taxation and Finance
Taxpayer Assistance Bureau
State Campus
Albany, New York 12227

New York State District Offices

For personal assistance, visit any of these offices:

Albany
30 Russell Road
at Westgate Shopping Center

Binghamton
State Office Building Annex
164 Hawley Street

Bronx
1375 Jerome Avenue

Brooklyn
141 Livingston Street

Buffalo
State Office Building
65 Court Street

Elmira
200 William Street

Harlem
State Office Building
163 West 125th Street

Kingston
Governor Clinton Hotel
1 Albany Avenue

Mineola
114 Old Country Road

New York
Two World Trade Center
63rd Floor

Plattsburgh
3 LaBarre Street

Queens
97 – 77 Queens Boulevard

Rochester
1 Marine Midland Plaza

Suffolk
State Office Building
Veterans Highway-Hauppauge

Syracuse
State Office Building
333 East Washington Street

Utica
State Office Building
207 Genesee Street

Watertown
State Office Building
317 Washington Street

White Plains
99 Church Street

City of New York

You can also get forms at these offices:

Bronx
City Collector's Office
Bergen Building
1932 Arthur Avenue

Brooklyn
Municipal Building
Room 1
Court and
Joralemon Streets

Manhattan
Municipal Building
Room 100 or
139 Centre Street
Room 110

Queens
City Collector's Office
90 – 15 Sutphin Boulevard
Jamaica

Staten Island
City Collector's Office
Room 200
350 St. Marks Place

(9/81) 3,800M (173)

Content. The form contains numerous difficult technical terms, for example, "catalytic agent credit," "lump-sum distribution," "accumulation-distribution credit."

Configuration. Bold black letters are used to identify the form. Its subheads, however, are obscured by using the lead word "Schedule" at the start of each heading. Coding is also largely neglected.

Print. Black on white provides excellent contrast. Print size and structure are good. While 10 point type is used on the face of the form, 8 point is used on the reverse side.

Organization. The double spacing used on the front of the form is easier to read than single-spaced sentences. However, the efficient use of space is severely compromised. Moreover, the reverse side of the form carries only general information on tax-rate schedules and office addresses and phone numbers. The form could well be combined with another appropriate form, and the information on the reverse side could be added to the instruction booklet.

State of New York Form MV 44, Driver License Application

This driver application form (exhibit L) is largely used for new applicants, since computer-processed renewal forms are sent out to currently licensed drivers.

Content. Section A on the reverse side carries technical class code numbers that are not readily understood.

Configuration. Large blue letters are used to identify the overall form. Subheadings, however, are not provided, nor is coding employed effectively.

Print. Blue print on light blue background yields very poor contrast. Also, print size is less than the minimum recommended, that is, 8 point size.

Organization. Items are sequentially numbered on the front page. Part B, however, could be better organized on a logical basis: (1) health, (2) criminal offenses, and (3) licensing history.

Fill-in. The instructions to use blue or black ink may not be heeded, since these may be interpreted to be only a preference. In this instance, the imperative "Do not" is more effective, for example, "*Do not* use pencil or other than black or blue ink."

Fill-in spaces appear to be adequate, but boxes to be checked are located to the left of the items. Group B responses on the reverse side could also be simplified with categories and boxes to be checked. Fill-in aids, such as partially filled-in dates or state designation (only New York is involved), could also be more effectively employed.

State of New York Form MV 82, Automobile Registration Application

This form is used primarily for new registrations (see exhibit M). Currently registered vehicles are forms-processed for renewal by computer.

Content. Sentences on the reverse side of the form are excessively wordy. For example, section F could be simplified to read as follows.

Check the boxes that apply to this vehicle:

1. Used only for transportation of household goods under I.C.C. or the Dept. of Transportation Authority ☐
   I.C.C. Permit No.____________________________
   Dept. of Transportation Authority
   Permit No. ____________________________
2. Used exclusively as a tank vehicle under Vehicle and Traffic Law Section 378. Attach Form MV-269 ☐
   (except in New York City)

EXHIBIT L
State of New York, Form MV-44, Application for Driver License

MV-44 (3/80)

State of New York - Department of Motor Vehicles

APPLICATION FOR DRIVER LICENSE

PLEASE PRINT WITH BLUE OR BLACK INK IN WHITE SPACES NEXT TO ARROWS.

BE SURE TO COMPLETE AND SIGN ON OTHER SIDE

FOR CENTRAL OFFICE USE ONLY
Batch File No.

1 Last Name — First — Middle Initial
Name

2 Date of Birth: Month — Day — Year — Sex M ☐ F ☐ — Proof Submitted
Birth/Sex

3 If you are presently a licensed New York driver, enter the motorist identification number exactly as it appears on your license.
MI

4 Number and Street (Mailing Address including Rural Delivery, Box No. and/or Apt. No.)
Street

5 City or Town — State
City/State

6 Zip Code — County of Residence
Zip — County

7 **Has your address changed since your last license was issued?** ☐ Yes ☐ No

8 Legal Address if different from Mailing Address

9 Height — **Restriction(s)**

10 Eye Color

Restrictions — Out of State OS

TO AMEND YOUR LICENSE, FILL IN THIS SECTION

a. For a change of name, print former name exactly as it appears on your present license.

Last Name — First — Middle Initial

b. For a change of license type FROM: ______ TO: ______

c. To ☐ add ☐ remove the following restriction:

d. **If other than above, give change and reason** ______

THIS COLUMN FOR OFFICE USE ONLY

RECIPROCITY	LRC
AMENDMENT	LAM
RENEWAL	LRN
DUPLICATE	LDP
NON REC'D ORIGINAL	LNO
ORIGINAL	LIS

LICENSE TYPE

	CLASS		CLASS
1	01	8	08
2	02	5LU	09
3	03	6LU	10
4	04	7A	7A
5	05	7B	7B
6	06	8A	8A
7	07	8B	8B

SPECIAL CONDITIONS

EXPIRED LICENSE	EL
MILITARY LICENSE	ML
NO-FEE	NF
RENEWAL-UPDATE	UP
UNCONDITIONAL	UC
UNRESTRICTED	UR
OUT OF STATE SURRENDER	VS

Fee $ — Expiration Date

Approved by

Issuing Office

Date

Validation Number

Stop Reason

Cashier Signature

EXHIBIT L (continued)
Form MV-44, reverse side

MV-44 (3/80)

ANSWER ALL QUESTIONS WHICH APPLY TO YOU

A

For persons applying for original Class 6, 6LU, 8, 8A or 8B Licenses

CONSENT OF PARENT OR GUARDIAN

I am the parent or guardian of the applicant named and I hereby consent to the issuance of a permit or license to said applicant.

Signature of Parent or Guardian ______________________ Relationship to Applicant ______________ Date __________

NOTE If you are 17 years old and have a Driver Education Blue Card (Form MV-285), consent is not required.

B

All applicants must answer all questions in this section.

For a duplicate, renewal or amended license, have the conditions mentioned below occurred since your last license was issued? For an original or reciprocity license, have the conditions mentioned ever occurred?

WRITE YES OR NO

1. Have you had or been treated for a convulsive disorder, epilepsy, fainting or dizzy spells, or any condition which caused unconsciousness? . . . . ______
2. Have you been treated for a heart ailment? . . . . ______
3. Have you had any mental illness for which you have been confined to a public or private institution or hospital? . . . . ______
4. Have you been confined to an institution or received treatment for narcotics addiction? . . . . ______

If you answered "Yes" to any of the questions above, obtain the appropriate Medical Statement form from your Motor Vehicle Issuing Office.

5. Do you have any hearing Impairment or other physical disability or have you suffered the loss of, or the loss of the use of, a leg, hand, foot or eye?. . . ______ ______

   If yes, give details:

WRITE YES OR NO

6. Have you ever held, or do you hold, a valid or renewable driver license issued by another State or Country? . . . . . . ______
   If "Yes", where issued ______
   Date of expiration: ______
7. Have you ever had a license, permit or license privilege to operate a motor vehicle refused, suspended, revoked or cancelled or an application for a Driver License denied in this State or elsewhere? . . . . ______
   If "Yes" has your license, permit or license privilege been restored or your application approved? . . . . ______
8. Have you been found guilty of ANY crime, offense, or traffic infraction (except parking violations), or forfeited bail in any court either in this State or elsewhere? . . . . ______
   If "Yes", give details below. If more space is needed, use Form MV-22.

Date	Crime,Infraction,Offense	Court & Location

C

Reciprocity

I request that the road test be waived based on my possession of the following current foreign license, OR out-of-state OR military license, which is current, or which has been expired for less than one year.

Type of License ______________________ This license was issued by the State or Country of ______________

Driver License No. ______________________ Expiration Date ______________

I certify that I was a permanent resident of the state or country in which the above license was issued at the time it was issued, that THE ABOVE LICENSE HAS BEEN IN EFFECT FOR AT LEAST 6 MONTHS, and that I have not failed a road test for a New York State driver license within the past 12 months. I understand that the waiver of the road test is at the discretion of the Commissioner of Motor Vehicles.

D

All Licenses

I, the undersigned, state that the information I have given on the foregoing application is true to the best of my knowledge and belief.

If a duplicate license is being applied for, I certify that I am the holder of a currently valid or renewable New York State Driver License that is not presently under suspension or revocation, and that this license has been lost, mutilated or destroyed. If the lost license is found after the duplicate license has been issued, I will surrender the lost license to the Department of Motor Vehicles and advise that a duplicate has been issued.

SIGN HERE **X** ______________________
Sign name in Full — A married woman must use her own first name.

FOR OFFICE USE ONLY — TEST RESULTS

				Applicant's Signature	Examiner's Signature
Eye Test	pass ☐		1		
Road Sign	pass ☐		2		
1st Written	pass ☐	fail ☐	3		
2nd Written	pass ☐	fail ☐	4		
1st Road Test	pass ☐	fail ☐	5		
2nd Road Test	pass ☐	fail ☐	6		

EXHIBIT M

State of New York, Application for Auto Registration or Title, Form MV-82

MV-82 (3/80)

State of New York - Department of Motor Vehicles

APPLICATION FOR REGISTRATION OR TITLE

PLEASE PRINT WITH BLUE OR BLACK INK IN WHITE SPACES NEXT TO ARROWS.

BE SURE TO COMPLETE AND SIGN ON OTHER SIDE

FOR CENTRAL OFFICE USE ONLY

Batch File No.

1 Last Name of Registrant | First | Middle Initial

2 Partner or Corporation Name or Legal Designation

Name

Name Cont'd.

3 Date of Birth | Month | Day | Year | Sex M ☐ F ☐ | **Proof Submitted**

Birth/Sex

4 Partner Date of Birth | Month | Day | Year | Sex M ☐ F ☐

5 Number and Street (Mailing Address - Include Rural Delivery, Box No. and/or Apt. No.)

Street

6 City or Town/State

City/State

7 Zip Code | County of Residence

Zip Code | **County**

8 Legal Address If Different

ENTER THE FOLLOWING INFORMATION FOR THE VEHICLE YOU ARE REGISTERING.

9 Vehicle Yr. | Make | Body Type | Color | Unladen Weight

10 Fuel/Cyl. | Type of Power ☐ Gas ☐ Diesel ☐ Electric | Cylinders | Max. Gross Weight | Adult Seating Capacity

11 Vehicle Identification Number | **MGW or Seating Capacity**

VI Number

12 Insurance Company | Ins. Co. Code | **Title/ Liens** | **Prior Owner**

Old Fee | **Old Expiration Date (RAC,RRN)** | **RR**

13 FOR A DUPLICATE, RENEWAL OR TRANSFER OF PLATES FILL IN THIS LINE. | Your Present Plate No. | Present Type of Registration | Present Exp. Date

QUESTIONS 14 & 15 APPLY TO 1973 AND NEWER VEHICLES ONLY.

OWNER OF VEHICLE IF NOT REGISTRANT (DIFFERENT OWNER)

14 Last Name | First | Middle Initial | Date of Birth

Number and Street | City | State | Zip Code

15 Vehicle was Purchased ☐ New ☐ Used | If Purchased New, Date of Sale ______

TO BE COMPLETED BY LICENSED NEW YORK STATE DEALER ONLY

16 **Lienholder's Name (If none, enter "None". If more than one, also use Section "G" on reverse.)**

Mailing Address - Number and Street | **City** | **State** | **Zip Code**

THIS COLUMN FOR OFFICE USE ONLY

☐ **Non-Transferable Registration**

☐ **Transferable Registration**

ORIGINAL ROR

RENEWAL RRN

ACTIVITY RAC

DUPLICATE RDP

Old Plate

Old Class

3 of Name

Expiration Date

New Plate

New Class | **CC**

SPECIAL CONDITIONS

AF	BV	CF	EX
FL	NE	NF	PA
RE	RP	RT	RV
SV	TO	TR	TX

SCOFFLAW CASE NO(S). (RRN)

Stk. No.

Fee Paid

Inspection Date | **Station No.**

Approved By

Date

Stop Reason

Cashier Signature

EXHIBIT M (continued)
Form MV-82, reverse side

MV-82 (3/80)

FILL OUT ALL SECTIONS BELOW WHICH APPLY TO YOU.

A. TO CERTIFY THAT YOUR VEHICLE WAS INSPECTED (FOR A DUPLICATE, RENEWAL, OR ORIGINAL REGISTRATION)

I certify that the vehicle was inspected on Mo.____Yr.___Certificate No.____________Station No.________

B. FOR REPLACEMENT OF REGISTRATION ITEMS

If you have lost any registration items or if they have been mutilated or destroyed, check below the items which need to be replaced:

☐ Registration Certificate ☐ Renewal Stub ☐ Sticker ☐ Plate: Lost Plate Number__________. ☐ one plate ☐ both plates

C. TO AMEND YOUR REGISTRATION

For a change of name, print your former name exactly as it is on your present registration: ______ Last ______ First ______ Middle Initial

For a change other than name, give reason for the change:

D. FOR SPECIAL REGISTRATIONS ONLY

a. If you are an amateur ham radio operator (not C.B.) licensed by the FCC to operate in New York State, list your Call Sign__________ Exp. Date__________

b. If you have plates in a series reserved for a special group, are you still eligible to receive them? ☐ Yes ☐ No
Do you have more than one set? ☐ Yes ☐ No
If "Yes", you must surrender or exchange all but one set for standard series plates.

E. FOR TRAILERS ONLY

This trailer will be used for ☐ Commercial ☐ Non-Commercial purposes.

F. CHECK ANY BOXES IN THIS SECTION WHICH APPLY FOR THIS VEHICLE

☐ It is used only in the transportation of household goods under I.C.C., or Dept. of Transportation authority.

☐ It is under Dept. of Transportation authority:
Permit Number __________

☐ It is under Interstate Commerce Commission authority:
I.C.C. Permit Number__________

☐ It is used exclusively as a tank vehicle in compliance with Section 378 of the Vehicle and Traffic Law.
Form MV-269 Tank Vehicle Compliance Certificate must be attached(except in New York City).

☐ It is used exclusively as an ambulance.
Check if: ☐ Fee is charged for carrying passengers.
☐ Used as an invalid coach or hearse.

☐ It is under government ownership.

☐ Junked Vehicle - Vehicle has been repaired and now meets all the requirements of Section 375 and 376 of the Vehicle and Traffic Law.

☐ It is used only as a Farm Vehicle (Form MV-260F must be attached).

☐ It is used only as an agricultural truck. (Form MV-259F must be attached.)

G. ADDITIONAL LIENHOLDERS – TO BE COMPLETED BY LICENSED NEW YORK STATE DEALER ONLY.

List any lienholders other than those specified on the front of this form.

Lienholder Name__________

Mailing Address__________ Number and Street ______ City ______ State ______ Zip Code

Lienholder Name__________

Mailing Address__________ Number and Street ______ City ______ State ______ Zip Code

H. I CERTIFY THAT:

1. The information given on this application is true.
2. There are no unsatisfied judgments against me as a result of a motor vehicle accident.
3. The registration is not currently under suspension or revocation.
4. The vehicle is fully equipped in accordance with the requirements of the Vehicle and Traffic Law.
5. There are no outstanding orders against me under the Finanacial Security Act.
6. If required, financial security is currently in effect.
7. If a farm vehicle registration, the vehicle will not be operated on a public highway except on the routes indicated on Form MV-260F (Certification of Farm Vehicle Routes).
8. If a passenger registration, passengers will not be carried for hire.
9. If plates are in a series reserved for a special group, I have only one set of these plates.
10. If a limited use vehicle registration, the vehicle will be operated subject to the restrictions contained in Section 2262 of the Vehicle and Traffic Law.

SIGN HERE **X** __________
Sign name in full. If not individual owner, give title.

DEALER CERTIFICATION - **This Certification must be signed even though "None" was entered as the answer to question 16 on the front of this form**

I certify that the lienholders listed on this form and supplementary forms filed herewith are the only recorded lienholders or lienholders who desire to perfect their security interests for this vehicle known to me. I take responsibility for the integrity of the papers delivered to the Motor Vehicle office.

____
Signature of Dealer or Power of Attorney

FOR OFFICE USE ONLY

a. For 1972 or older leased vehicles, an MV-95 was submitted and the proof returned to applicant. Date__________Examiner__________

b. Out-of-State Title__________

Configuration. Different modes of coding could be effectively applied for easy recognition of the form and its sections. For example, a trailer silhouette could be used at the upper left area of Section E, a yellow color code could be employed for Section H to highlight the certification requirements, and so on.

Print. Dark green on lighter green yields poor visual contrast for office use. Print size is also less than the 8 point size recommended, while the stroke-width ratio to character height on the reverse side of the form is also less than recommended for good readability.

Organization. Items are consecutively numbered on the front and alphabetized on the back. Several reverse-side items are not sequenced, however. Some items are also vague, such as "adult seating capacity," which would yield unreliable information.

Fill-in. Spaces generally appear adequate for fill-in responses. Fill-in boxes are located to the left of the items, so the right hand obscures the text during the fill-in exercise. Fill-in aids are also neglected, for example partial date and the state (only "New York" is possible) might have been printed in on item 6.

State of New York Form MV-500, Learner's Permit

This is a multicopy form, using carbon paper for duplication of name, address, identification, and signature (exhibit N). The form generally appears to have good readability, with black on white contrast and 8 point type size. Sentences on road testing are lengthy, and many of them have multiple verbs and conjunctions. The negative term "will not" is appropriately used for emphasis.

Fill-in boxes, except for test results, are to the left of the items. The hand thus blocks the items during fill-in.

EXHIBIT N

State of New York, Learner's Permit, Form MV-500

MV-500 (2/79) State of New York - Department of Motor Vehicles

Restrictions

PART 1 LEARNER'S PERMIT (Read Reverse Side)

PLEASE TYPE OR PRINT - USE BALL POINT PEN - PRESS HARD

Name	Last	First	M.I.	
No. & Street				
City, State & ZIP Code				
	Date of Birth	Height	Sex	Eye Color
	Applicant's Signature - DO NOT PRINT - Sign Name In Full			

OFFICE USE ONLY
CIRCLE CLASS DESIRED

1	5	7	8
2	5LU	7A	8A
3	6	7B	8B
4	6LU		

Also licensed as:

Application Filing Fee - $5.00

Learner's Permit Not Valid in Road Test Areas.

TEMPORARY LICENSE ENDORSEMENT SUPERSEDES LEARNER'S PERMIT ENDORSEMENT	"Temporary License Endorsement"	"Learner's Permit Endorsement"	Validation Number and Date

→

YOU WILL NOT BE GIVEN A ROAD TEST UNLESS –

1. Your vehicle has a valid Inspection Certificate (not required for Class B or C limited use motorcycle) and is in good working condition.
2. You have the registration to all vehicles to be used in connection with the road test.
3. Your accompanying driver has a valid license on his person.
4. If taking the motorcycle or limited use motorcycle road test, you provide a car and a licensed driver so that the Inspector can observe the traffic portion of the road test.
5. You have the following forms:
   a. Application for Driver License (Form MV-44T)
   b. Road Test Appointment Stub (Form MV-500, Part 2)
   c. New York Learner's Permit (Form MV-500, Part 1)
6. You are on time.

☐ **NOTICE OF FAILURE IN ROAD TEST –**

☐ Test No. 1. You may apply for your 2nd road test if it has been less than one year since you filed your current Application for a Driver License.

Mail or bring this form to your local Motor Vehicle Office for a new road test date.

☐ Test No. 2. If you still desire a driver license, you must submit this form, a new Form MV-44T Application for Driver License and a new Form MV-500 Request for Learner's Permit and Tests. You will be required to pay the $5 fee. If this is done within 30 days of failure date, and if this is your first renewal, preliminary tests are waived.

☐ **NOTICE OF PASSING OF ROAD TEST –**

1. Enclosed is your Temporary License. After 45 days, if you have not received your new license application, notify your Motor Vehicle office immediately.
2. The Temporary License and subsequent licenses issued after passing a road test are subject to a 6-month probationary period which begins on the date of issuance of the Temporary License.
3. THE TEMPORARY LICENSE AND/OR CURRENT LICENSE MUST BE SUBMITTED WHEN THE NEW LICENSE APPLICATION IS SUBMITTED FOR A VALIDATION.

☐ **NOTICE OF PASSING OF ROAD TEST - AMENDMENT OF CURRENT LICENSE UPON PAYMENT OF FEE**

Return to this office with your current license and all enclosed papers. Your new license will then be issued to you.

TEST RESULTS

			Applicant's Signature	Examiner's Signature
Eye Test	pass ☐			
Road Sign	pass ☐			
1st Written	pass ☐	fail ☐		
2nd Written	pass ☐	fail ☐		

WHY ASSESS GOVERNMENT FORMS?

Government agencies that issue forms are bureaucracies and, by definition, responsive primarily to internal pressures and exigencies. The sample forms and evaluation exercises in this chapter would be of little significance if bureaucratic organizations were totally insensitive to public complaints and scrutiny.

Bureaucracies are committed to efficiency, however, and strive toward complete internal competence. Inconsistent forms, or those that collect unreliable and incomplete data, are not acceptable to an efficient bureaucrat. Government-designed forms must gather necessary and complete information or fail in the basic bureaucratic mission. Therein lies the major impetus for forms inprovement within bureaucracies.

External political pressures are not without influence. A political awareness of diminishing national productivity is heightened by national paperwork overkill. It is estimated that 1.5 billion man-hours are spent in filling out forms, which is more than is expended annually in automobile production. This realization has brought renewed concern about paperwork excesses and the need for efficiency in government forms design.

SUMMARY

Government agencies are characterized as bureaucratic, hence they are less likely than private business to respond to appeals by respondents to simplify forms. However, when forms fail to capture complete and reliable information due to poor design, the bureaucratic process is threatened, which provides impetus for forms inprovement. External political pressures can also be effectively applied to induce the bureaucracy to change badly designed forms.

A number of commonly used federal and state government forms are presented in this chapter for human-factors critique, including those of the U.S. Internal Revenue Service, the U.S. Postal Service, New York State Department of Taxation and Finance, and the New York State Department of Motor Vehicles.

CHAPTER 7
An Evaluation of Business-Form Applications and Design

Business organizations, as outlined in table 6.1, differ from government agencies both in operational objectives and success criteria. Financial success is the ultimate goal of the business enterprise, while orderly survival continues to be the primary goal of the government agency.

Financial success can be achieved only by efficient management of resources and effective competition in the marketplace. Stated succinctly, a business-success formula is one that minimizes operational costs while maximizing profits. Forms application and design efficiency thus become crucial considerations in the effective performance of business organizations.

FORM APPLICATIONS

Figure 7.1 outlines three operational phases within a business in which forms are used. The promotion-and-intake

FIGURE 7.1
Operational phases during which business forms are applied.

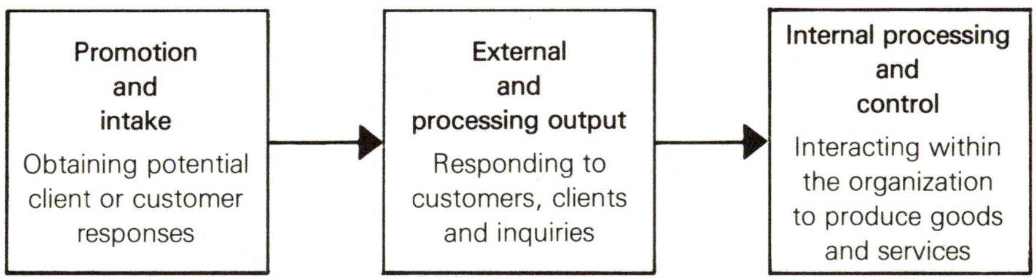

phase requires responses from prospects or clients to expand the marketing activity. External processing and output involves the use of forms for prompt and efficient responses to inquiries, complaints, purchase orders, and the like. Internal processing and control uses forms to help maintain operational efficiency within the organization.

PROMOTION AND INTAKE

This phase of business operation usually generates the greatest volume of forms usage. Forms are used at this stage to obtain potential sales leads and to solicit prospective customer responses for other specific purposes depending on the nature of the business.

The quality of the form may determine in part whether or not a potential client or customer will choose to respond—that is, a poorly designed form could be regarded as too much trouble to fill out or too difficult to understand.

Whenever a form is used, it should have been predetermined that it is the best way to obtain the information or lead, as compared with personal or phone contact, for instance. After use of a form has been decided on, the design should be proven effective in eliciting the desired responses.

Following are examples and critiques of a number of promotion and intake forms.

A Textbook Review Form

This form (exhibit O) is a brief and somewhat open-ended questionnaire that is attached to an explanatory form letter. A more structured format might reduce required response time and further encourage a prospect to respond to the questions. For example, the following format would simplify response requirements:

EXAMINATION COPY SENT: (Date and title filled in by publisher) ______________________

Please check (✓) or complete each question as indicated below.

REVIEW INTEREST: Basic Text ☐
Supplemental Text ☐

REVIEW DECISION: Accepted ☐ No. Ordered ________
Still Being Considered ☐ By ________
Rejected ☐

Please comment briefly on the strengths and weaknesses of the book: ______________________

____

A Form Used to Interest Stockholders in Available Products

Exhibit P is a form sent to stockholders to encourage them to order products produced by the company.

Content. The introductory paragraph is made up of complex sentences that make for poor readability. The word "authoritative" may also be difficult for some of the respondents to understand.

Configuration. Use of a form title would facilitate an appreciation of the form's intent, for example, "Product Information Available to Stockholders." Pictorial coding could also be used to simplify recognition of product groups.

EXHIBIT O
A form used to obtain response to textbook review requests.

Title or description of course for which this text was considered:

____

____

Text previously or currently used: __________________________

Examination was for ______ a basic text; ______ a supplementary text.

Text sent for examination:

______ will be used.

______ order has been sent for ______ copies by ____________

______ order for approx. ______ copies will be placed by __________

______ will not be used.

______ is still under consideration.

Please state briefly the features of the book, or other reasons, which caused it either to be selected for use or not selected:

____

____

Print. The print is small, 8 point size. A larger size would more adequately accommodate elderly respondents.

Organization. Logical categorical product grouping is used. The "other products" group could be better arranged, however, into heating, ventilation, and lighting. The "full horsepower" item also needs clarification.

Fill-in. Fill-in boxes are located to the left of the items, blocking their view during the fill-in exercise. These should be on the right side. Also, fill-in aids are neglected. For example, if taken from a computerized list of stockholders, the names and addresses could have been filled in.

A Form Used to Obtain Automobile Insurance Sales Leads

This form (exhibit Q) is attached to a form letter. It is attractively designed with white on blue headings.

Content. Items 9 and 10 contain multiple conditions within a sentence that require a yes-or-no response. Respondents

EXHIBIT P
A form used to interest stockholders in available products.

As you know, your Company makes numerous products for the home, and as a share owner of __________ you may be considering the purchase of one or more of them at this time or in the near future. If you would like to receive authoritative information on any of these products, please check the appropriate items below and return this form in the enclosed envelope.

HOUSEWARES
__ Air Coolers
__ Air Purifiers
__ Automatic Blankets
__ Automatic Tooth Brush
__ Baby Food Warmers
__ Can Openers
__ Clocks
__ Coffee Makers
__ De-Humidifiers
__ Fans
__ Floor Polishers
__ Floor Washer-Dryers
__ Grill and Waffle Baker
__ Hair Dryers
__ Heaters, Portable
__ Heating Pads
__ Irons
__ Kettle
__ Knife Sharperers
__ Mixers
__ Rotisseries
__ Saucepans
__ Skillets
__ Toasters
__ Vacuum Cleaners
__ Vaporizers

MAJOR APPLIANCES
__ Air Conditioners, Room
__ Dishwashers
__ Disposall® —food waste disposers
__ Dryers
__ Freezers
__ Kitchen Cabinets
__ Ranger and Cooktops
__ Refrigerators
__ Wall Ovens
__ Washers
__ Water Heaters

HOME ENTERTAINMENT PRODUCTS
Radios:
__ Portable
__ Table
__ Clock
__ Intercoms
__ Educational Project Kits
Phonographs:
__ Portable
__ Console
Television:
__ Black & White
__ Color

OTHER PRODUCTS
__ Central Air-Conditioners
—residential & commercial
__ "Full Housepower"
__ Heating Cable Sets
__ Heating Systems —electric—baseboard, embedded wire, wall-mounted
__ Lamps & Lighting
__ Remote Control Wiring
__ Textolite®
—plastic counter, cabinet & wall surfacing
__ Wall Switches and Plates
__ Warm Air Furnaces

ADDITIONAL INFORMATION

Other Products ______________________________
____
____
____
____

Please print your name ______________________________

and address ______________________________
____

EXHIBIT Q
A Form Used to Obtain Leads for Automobile Insurance Sales

FREE AUTO RATE QUOTATION REQUEST FORM

Please print answers to all questions, send no money, complete this form, mail in enclosed envelope today.

1. Name of current insurance company: ____________
2. Date present insurance expires: Mo. ________ Yr. ________
3. Employer: ____________
4. Title/Grade: ____________ # of Yrs. ______
5. If in present occupation less than 2 yrs. or retired, give former occupation: ____________
6. Years at current address ____________
7. Have you previously been insured with ☐ Yes ☐ No
8. Phone: Bus. (____)________ Home (____)________
9. Has any driver had a license suspended or revoked, or been convicted of driving under the influence of drugs or alcohol? ☐ Yes** ☐ No
10. Has any driver had any accidents, regardless of fault, and/or convictions for traffic violations in the past five years? ☐ Yes** ☐ No

**If Yes, please give details in the space provided on back of form.

auto insurance not available in Massachusetts or New Jersey.

Do we have your correct name & address?

DRIVER INFORMATION:

LIST ALL DRIVERS (including yourself)	RELATION	BIRTHDATE Mo.	Day	Yr.	Marital Status	Male Female	OCCUPATION	% of Use for Each Driver Car #1	Car #2	Car #3	Driver Training Yes	No	Yrs. Driving
1.	Self										☐	☐	
2.											☐	☐	
3.											☐	☐	
4.											☐	☐	

If student is away at school, give distance from home: ________ Miles

AUTOMOBILE INFORMATION:

CAR	YEAR	Make (Buick, Dodge, etc.)	MODEL (Skylark, Omni, etc.)	BODY TYPE (2 Door, Conv., etc.)	# Cylinders	Est. Total Mileage on Car	Est. Annual Mileage	Days a week driven to work, school or depot	One way distance	Is car used in employment except to and from work? Yes*	No	Car location if different from mail address City, State, Zip
1.										☐	☐	
2.										☐	☐	
3.										☐	☐	

*If Yes, explain ____________

Note: Should you not meet underwriting requirements, you may still obtain the same quality auto coverage and service from one of our affiliates, at somewhat higher rates.

Check for information on: Homeowners Insurance ☐ Boatowners Insurance ☐ Overseas ☐

Signature ____________ Date ____________ P-370 (3-82)

frequently give unreliable or incomplete responses to such items.

Configuration. The form title provides for good recognition of its intent. Modes of coding, however, could be introduced to improve item recognition. For example, items 9 and 10 could be color coded yellow to highlight violations and accidents, the different numbered cars could be colored differently for easy line tracking, and so on.

Print. The black on white print provides excellent contrast. The print is 8 point, the minimum recommended size.

Organization. A logical order is generally indicated, though items 1 to 10 are somewhat broken in sequence. Item 8 concerns phone numbers, which would be better grouped with employment and resident information rather than with insurance information.

Fill-in. The name and address are already filled in with computer word processing techniques. Fill-in spaces are too small for names of drivers to be listed under driver information. Space to fill in the car location is also insufficient.

A Form Used to Screen Preferred Borrowers

This form (exhibit R) is given to preferred bank customers seeking a loan. The reverse side of the form simulates an engraved invitation to "Selected Income People."

Content. Use of the term "preferentials" may lack clarity. The last sentence at the bottom of the form concerning rate of charge is also unclear. The abbreviation "a/c#" is uncommon. "Regular and "Special" pertaining to checking accounts may also not be clearly understood by respondents.

Configuration. The form is attractive, with a quickly identifiable purpose. Subheadings, however, are not effectively

EXHIBIT R
A Form Used to Screen Preferred Borrowers

Confidential Loan for *The Preferentials*

Purpose of Loan ______________________

Date..........

Name.......... Age..........

Home Address (Street).......... How Long?.......... Yrs.

City.......... State.......... ZIP #.......... Phone No..........

Previous Address.......... City.......... State..........

Married?.......... Name of Wife (or Husband).......... No. of dependents..........

Name of Firm with which you are connected..........

Business Address.......... City.......... State.......... ZIP #..........

Your Position.......... Business Phone No..........

How long with firm.......... Salary $..........

Amount of other income $.......... Source..........

....

At what Bank do you carry a checking account?..........
☐ Regular ☐ Special

Branch of Bank..........

LIST ALL INSTALLMENT DEBTS (Loans—Purchases etc.) IF NONE, STATE NONE ....

To Whom Due	Original Amount	Monthly Payments	Balance Due	To Whom Due	Original Amount	Monthly Payments	Balance Due
....	$..........	$..........	$..........	....	$..........	$..........	$..........
....	$..........	$..........	$..........	....	$..........	$..........	$..........

Do you have a Check-Credit Line at any Bank?.......... If so, please indicate:

Name of Bank.......... Monthly Payment.......... Bal. Due..........

Do you own an Auto?.......... Year.......... Make..........

Financed by:.......... Address.......... Bal. Due..........

Total indebtedness exclusive of mortgages and loans fully secured by stocks and bonds $..........

If None State None.......... Are there any judgments or legal proceedings against you?..........

Location of Real Estate you own..........

Value $.......... Mortgage $.......... Mortgage Payment per Month $..........

If Home not owned, please give monthly rental $ ....

Have you ever borrowed or financed anything through this bank?.......... $^a/_c$#..........

ACTUAL AMOUNT OF CASH WANTED $..........

I wish to pay in 12 mo. ☐ 15 mo. ☐ 18 mo. ☐ 24 mo. ☐ 30 mo. ☐ 36 mo. ☐
60 mo. ☐ (Property Modernization Loan.)

I wish mail sent to: Home Address ☐ Business Address ☐

I prefer to make payments on or about ....
(Please indicate date of month most convenient for you)

Social Security No.

____

....
Signature

The rate of charge for this loan does not exceed six dollars per annum discount per one hundred dollars face amount of loan.

employed, nor is coding. Color coding, for example, could be used for personal-and-employment information by printing in green and financial history could be in blue.

Print. Print is 10 point size, with good black-on-white reading contrast. The small print at the bottom, however, is substandard.

Organization. Organization seems to be adequate. A more logical arrangement of personal, employment, credit, and financial information could be provided. Numbering of items would also enhance the organization.

Fill-in. Entry-space allowances are not in keeping with maximum fill-in requirements. Installment debt information spaces are crowded, while a 1½ inch space is provided for a yes-no response to a check-credit line question. Fill-in boxes are located to the right for right-hand response on all but the bank checking-account question. Dollar sign fill-in aids are also lacking on a number of items.

Direct-Mail Form Used to Solicit Borrowers

Exhibit S is a form sent direct mail to obtain leads on potential borrowers. It is attached to a form letter.

Content. The terms used generally seem to be familiar. "Disclose," however, may not be understood by some respondents, nor is the abbreviation "Mo Pmts" a common one. A conditional negative statement made concerning alimony may be difficult to understand.

Configuration. The form lacks a descriptive heading with a statement of purpose. The first section also lacks a heading, and color could be effectively employed to provide easy visual grouping—perhaps green for personal history, blue for assets, and yellow for liabilities.

EXHIBIT S

A Form Used to Arouse Interest in Potential Borrowers

MINIMUM LOAN $5,000
PLEASE PRINT
NOTE: INCOMPLETE APPLICATIONS WILL NOT BE PROCESSED.

Number of repayment months (circle one) 12 24 36

I would like the loan check issued* and mailed:
immediately ☐ on the following date ______

*Finance charges are calculated from the date the check is issued. First payment will not be due until 45 days after the date the check is issued.

Optional Credit Life Insurance Yes ☐ No ☐

My Social Security Number is: ☐☐☐ ☐☐ ☐☐☐☐

Date of birth: ______

My home address is: Street ______

City ______ State ______ Zip ______

Yrs. There ______ Phone ( ) ______

Business or Employer ______ Yrs. there* ______

Street ______ Phone ( ) ______

City ______ State ______ Zip ______

Position or Occupation ______

My current annual income $ ______

Other Income $ ______ Source: ______

Note: you need not disclose alimony, child support, separate maintenance income or its source, unless you want us to consider it.

*If less than 2 years please name previous business or employer:

Previous Business or Employer ______ Yrs. there ______

Street ______

City ______ State ______ Zip ______

Position or Occupation ______ Income $ ______

Mo. Rent $ ______ or Mtge. $ ______ Rental income $ ______

Mortgage balance $ ______ Original amt. $ ______

Mortgage holder ______

Address ______

Total credit outstanding $ ______ Mo. Pmts. $ ______
(other than mortgage)

Personal checking account Bank: ______

Address ______ Balance $ ______

Savings Account Bank ______

Address ______ Balance $ ______

If self-employed, Business Bank ______

Address ______

Please send mail to my home ☐ office ☐

I have received and read the enclosed credit terms and conditions.

______
(Please print) First name M.I. Last name

(Signature) ______

To reach me quickly, call ______
(Area code) Telephone No.

between the hours of ______ and ______ AM. PM.

OVER $10,000

Tell us about your financial situation.
PLEASE PRINT

ASSETS

TYPE OF ASSET	DESCRIPTION OF ASSET	PRESENT VALUE
Business Checking Acct.		$
Personal Checking Acct.		$
Savings Acct.		$
Automobiles	Make Year	$
		$
Real Estate: Address	Type Property Date Acquired Purchase Cost	
	$	$
	$	$
Stocks and Bonds	Type: Stocks—S Bonds—B Issuer	$
		$
		$
Cash Surrender Value of Life Insurance	Issuer Policy Face Value $	$
	$	$
Other Financial Assets	Describe in Detail	$
		$
Total Assets		$

LIABILITIES

TYPE OF LIABILITY	DESCRIPTION OF LIABILITY	PRESENT BALANCE
Personal Loans	Lender	$
		$
		$
Credit Cards	Maximum Credit Line $	$
	$	$
Visa/Master Card	Maximum Credit Line $	$
	$	$
Bank Lines of Credit	Maximum Credit Line $	$
	$	$
Mortgages: Name and Address of Creditor		$
Property Address	Original Balance $	$
	$	$
	$	$
Other Debts	Describe in Detail	$
		$
Total Liabilities		$

Print. The print size is substandard, though good black-on-white contrast is provided. Many elderly respondents would find the small print difficult to read.

Organization. Grouping of information items generally is logical. Items about renting or owning a home might be better grouped with other personal data items. Consecutive numbering of items would also help both in reading and in filling out the form. Some clutter is also evident in the assets group.

Fill-in. Space allowance is crowded for the real estate items and other assets under the assets group. Vertical lines used for the Social Security number fill-in space have been found to detract from fill-in and reading efficiency. Fill-in boxes are aptly located to the right of items for right-hand fill-in.

A Form Used to Solicit Journal Subscriptions

Exhibit T shows a form that is mailed to association members to solicit their subscriptions to professional journals.

Content. The passive voice is used to indicate the single-copy restriction of the form. Active voice would be more effective, for example, "Order only single copies of these selected publications on this form. Make quantity orders through the Order Department." Code letters and numbers included to the right of the amount columns may be confusing. These should be explained, for example, "for office use only."

Configuration. The purpose of the form is obscured; not until the fourth line from the top is the purpose described. Also, coding could be more effectively employed, for instance, "Write in the price for each item you order" could be color coded blue on a bright yellow strip to highlight required action.

EXHIBIT T
1982 Publication Order Form, American Psychological Association

AMERICAN PSYCHOLOGICAL ASSOCIATION
1200 SEVENTEENTH STREET, N.W.
WASHINGTON, D.C. 20036
1982 PUBLICATIONS ORDER FORM
FOR APA FELLOWS, MEMBERS AND ASSOCIATES
PAYMENT DUE FEBRUARY 15, 1982
Dues, billed separately, automatically provide subscriptions to *American Psychologist* and *APA Monitor*

MEMBER NUMBER	DUES CODE	APA STATUS

WRITE IN THE PRICE FOR EACH ITEM YOU ORDER

SELECTED APA PUBLICATIONS	PRICE	AMOUNT	
ACTIVITIES HANDBOOK FOR THE TEACHING OF PSYCHOLOGY	$ 9 00	$	30
AGING IN THE 1980s	19 50		31
AMERICAN PSYCHOLOGY IN HISTORICAL PERSPECTIVE	15 00		32
APA'S GUIDE TO RESEARCH SUPPORT	16 00		33
CAREER OPPORTUNITIES FOR PSYCHOLOGISTS Expanding and Emerging Areas	6 00		34
GRADUATE STUDY IN PSYCHOLOGY 1982-1983	7 00		35
PREPARING FOR GRADUATE STUDY (NOT FOR SENIORS ONLY!)	6 50		36
PSYCHOLOGY AND NATIONAL HEALTH INSURANCE A SOURCEBOOK	15 00		37
THE PSYCHOLOGY MAJOR Training and Employment Strategies	10 00		38
PSYCHOLOGY TEACHER'S RESOURCE BOOK	9 00		39
PUBLICATION MANUAL OF THE APA 2ND ED	8 00		40
RESOURCES IN ENVIRONMENT AND BEHAVIOR	10 00		41
THESAURUS OF PSYCHOLOGICAL INDEX TERMS 3RD ED (available early 1982)	40 00		43
WHO IS THE CLIENT?	7 50		44
G STANLEY HALL LECTURE SERIES VOL 1	8 50		45
PsycINFO RETROSPECTIVE Learning and Communication Disorders An Abstracted Bibliography 1971-1980 (available early 1982)	25 00		46
PsycINFO RETROSPECTIVE Mental Retardation An Abstracted Bibliography 1971-1980 (available early 1982)	25 00		47
1982 APA MEMBERSHIP REGISTER (available spring 1982)	9 00		90
1981 DIRECTORY OF THE APA	30 00		91
SELECTED APA PUBLICATIONS SUBTOTAL (Add prices for items ordered)		$	

ONLY SINGLE COPIES OF THE SELECTED PUBLICATIONS MAY BE ORDERED ON THIS FORM
PLEASE CONTACT THE APA ORDER DEPARTMENT FOR QUANTITY PURCHASES

SPECIAL 20% DISCOUNT ON 1982 APA JOURNALS & SELECTED PUBLICATIONS

PLEASE RETURN THIS ORDER FORM WITH REMITTANCE

Signature ______________________ Date __________

1982 APA JOURNAL SUBSCRIPTIONS ORDER
PRICES FOR CONTINUING YOUR 1981 SUBSCRIPTIONS ARE PREPRINTED. TO CANCEL A SUBSCRIPTION, CROSS OUT THE PREPRINTED 1982 SUBSCRIPTION PRICE. TO ADD NEW SUBSCRIPTIONS, WRITE IN THE PRICE FOR EACH ITEM YOU ORDER

JOURNALS	PRICE	1982 SUBSCRIPTIONS	
CONTEMPORARY (Monthly)	15.00		CT
ABNORMAL (Bimonthly)	17.00		AB
APPLIED (Bimonthly)	19.00		AL
COMPARATIVE (Bimonthly)	20.00		CM
CONSULTING & CLINICAL (Bimonthly)	25.00		CS
EDUCATIONAL (Bimonthly)	20.00		ED
BULLETIN (Bimonthly)	25 00		BU
COUNSELING (Bimonthly)	14.00		CO
REVIEW (Bimonthly)	12.00		RV
PERSONALITY & SOCIAL (Monthly)	35 00		PS
DEVELOPMENTAL (Bimonthly)	20.00		DV
PROFESSIONAL (Bimonthly)	20 00		PR
EXPERIMENTAL (JEP) All Four Journals	45.00		XJ
JEP GENERAL (Quarterly)	10.00		XG
JEP LEARNING MEMORY & COGNITION (Bimonthly)	15.00		XL
JEP HUMAN PERCEPTION (Bimonthly)	15.00		XP
JEP ANIMAL BEHAVIOR (Quarterly)	10.00		XA
JSAS Catalog of Selected Documents (Quarterly)	6.00		JS
PSYCHOLOGICAL ABSTRACTS (Issues only monthly)	125.00		P1
PSYCHOLOGICAL ABSTRACTS Issues (Monthly) Indexes (s-annual)	225.00		P2
PsycSCAN LD MR (Quarterly)	10 00		P6
PsycSCAN Applied (Quarterly)	10 00		P5
PsycSCAN Clinical (Quarterly)	10 00		P3
PsycSCAN Developmental (Quarterly)	10 00		P4

(A) JOURNAL SUBSCRIPTION SUBTOTAL (Add prices for items ordered)	$
(B) ENTER AMOUNT FOR SELECTED PUBLICATIONS	$
(C) PUBLICATIONS TOTAL (Add lines A & B)	$
(D) MULTIPLY LINE (C) X .20	–
TOTAL AMOUNT PAYABLE (Subtract line D from C)	$

Make check payable, in U.S. dollars, to the American Psychological Association
SEE INSTRUCTIONS ON REVERSE SIDE

DO NOT DETACH THIS SECTION, RETURN ENTIRE FORM.

NAME AND ADDRESS CHANGES

MEMBER NUMBER

Name & Address on Record

Enter changes or corrections below.
(Please leave the name line blank unless it is to be corrected)

Name:
Address:

Zip Code:

APA DUES AND SUBSCRIPTIONS MAY BE TREATED AS DEDUCTIONS ON YOUR INCOME TAX RETURNS.

Print. The type size is less than recommended, with some as small as 5 point. This might be barely readable by older respondents. Blue-green print is used, which yields poor contrast. The upper case type used for instructions is also less readable than upper and lower case.

Organization. The order is good, with publications on the left and journals on the right. The caveat to order only single copies, however, would be better placed at the top so it can be read before erroneous entries might have been made.

Fill-in. Fill-in aids are good. Membership and current subscription data (not shown) are printed out on the form.

Typical Bank Deposit and Withdrawal Forms

Deposit forms are illustrated (exhibit U) for savings accounts and checking accounts. A withdrawal order is illustrated for a savings account.

Content. The checking account deposit ticket contains a technical reference to a uniform commercial code. More simple terms would improve readability, for example, "All checks must be cleared before account is credited." The savings account withdrawal order contains an admonition, "Do not cash," which is equivocal.

Configurations. Both the checking and savings account tickets fail to identify the type of account, that is, checking or savings. A subhead for listing of checks is also poorly presented on the checking account form. Color coding could be more effectively employed. The "Bank use only" section on the withdrawal order, for example, could be set off by another color than that used for the customer.

Print. Good contrast is provided with black or dark brown print on white background for the checking account deposit

EXHIBIT U

Typical Deposit and Withdrawal Tickets

Date: ____/____/19 ____

ACCOUNT NO.: ____________

NAME: ____________
(Please Print)

ADDRESS: ____________

This deposit is accepted subject to the rules and regulations of this bank, and the terms and conditions upon the reverse hereof

(See Other Side)

	Dollars	Cents
BILLS		
SILVER		
CHECKS Please endorse all checks and drafts. List local checks by name of bank. Out-of-town checks by name of city		
TOTAL $		

B-1 REV 12/76

DEPOSIT TICKET

DATE 19

CHECKS AND OTHER ITEMS ARE RECEIVED FOR DEPOSIT SUBJECT TO THE PROVISIONS OF THE UNIFORM COMMERCIAL CODE OR ANY APPLICABLE COLLECTION AGREEMENT

DEPOSITED IN

Savings Bank
New York

CASH → LIST CHECKS SINGLY		
TOTAL FROM OTHER SIDE		
TOTAL ITEMS TOTAL		

50-7088
2213 o

USE OTHER SIDE FOR ADDITIONAL LISTING
ENTER TOTAL HERE

BE SURE EACH ITEM IS PROPERLY ENDORSED

⑆2213708 8⑆ 838 0008105⑈ 0451

SAVINGS ACCOUNT WITHDRAWAL ORDER

ACCOUNT NO. ____________

DATE ____________ 19 ____

PAY TO ____________ **OR BEARER $** ____________
(Please Print)

____________ **DOLLARS**
(Write Amount in Words)

CASH ____ CK. ____
M.O. ____ DFT. ____
(Bank Use Only)

DO NOT CASH

SIGNATURE ____________

ADDRESS ____________
(Notify Teller of Any Change in Your Address)

REV 10/77 B-2

ticket and the savings account withdrawal order. Poorer contrast, green on white, is used for the savings account deposit form. Type is 8 point or larger on all but the checking account deposit slips, which has substandard size. The latter also employs all capital letters, which are less readable than upper- and lower-case letters.

Organization. Sequence is logical on all three forms, although the savings account deposit form could reduce "bills and silver" to "cash." The savings account withdrawal order format becomes confusing where the instructional words are underlined along with the fill-in space.

Fill-in. The space allowance for check listings on the checking account deposit ticket may be insufficient. Fill-in aids are generally good, with dates and dollar signs included as partial fill-ins.

A Form Used to Obtain Publisher Survey Data

Exhibit V shows a form enclosed with a letter requesting information for a survey on the book production industry.

Content. The form contains complex sentences, which could be simplified to enhance readability. Negative terms could be changed to positive. Items 1 and 2 could be simplified to enhance readability.

Configuration. A heading is needed to explain the overall content.

Print. Typewritten copy was reproduced using offset printing. Thus, character stroke-to-height ratio is not optimal.

Organization. The development generally appears to be logical, proceeding from manuscript questions to those concerning publication.

EXHIBIT V

A form used to request publisher survey data.

NOTE: There is no provision for company or personal name. If you wish to include yours, please do so. Our basic interest is with accurate data, however, not names. If someone in your organization, in addition to yourself, should also receive this form for reply, please photocopy this, or else request additional forms from us.

YOUR TITLE: ....

1. Does your company create original manuscripts in-house that are eventually used for or as publications or periodicals?

   Yes ( )
   No ( )

2. Do you contract with outside authors to create such publications?

   Yes ( )
   No ( )

3. Do you produce publications at the following periods:

   Daily ( ) Quarterly ( ) Annually ( )
   Weekly ( ) Semi Annually ( ) Other (specify) ____________

4. What kind of publication do you produce?

	Avg. No. of Pages/Issue Or Title	No. of Issues or New Title Year	How Bound*	Are these produced by: Commercial Printer	In-Plant Shop in Own Company
Operating & Specification manuals	________	________	____	( )	( )
Sales Manuals	________	________	____	( )	( )
Catalogs	________	________	____	( )	( )
Annual Reports	________	________	____	( )	( )
Company Magazines	________	________	____	( )	( )
Prestige volumes for public relations	________	________	____	( )	( )
Miscellaneous booklets	________	________	____	( )	( )
Proceedings of meetings	________	________	____	( )	( )
Monographs	________	________	____	( )	( )
Reference volumes	________	________	____	( )	( )
Other (specify)	________	________	____	( )	( )

*Please indicate binding by this simple code:

Looseleaf, ringbinders	LL	Wire-stitched, stapled	WR
Adhesive, glued	AD	Hard cover, casebound	HC
Plastic, wire, comb, mechanical	PL	Paperback, softcover	PB

Fill-in. Fill-in spaces are below or to the right of items, providing for convenient fill-in action. Item 4 might be better structured to permit a simple checking response to list the kinds of publications produced. Reference material is on the same side of the form as the items to be filled in, thus providing for an efficient response.

A Form Used for Personal-Data Survey

Exhibit W is a form attached to a letter which advises the recipient that he or she is being listed in the publication *Who's Who in the East.* It solicits biographical information.

Content. Items are brief and succinctly describe information that is needed. The negative "do not" is also appropriately used for emphasis.

Configuration. The heading that describes the purpose of the form, "Biographical Data," could be given more prominence. Size and color coding could be employed more effectively to highlight headings and item groups.

Print. Type is 8 point size. Respondents with poor vision might prefer larger print.

Organization. The categories in which items are listed should be improved. Professional and career items, for example, are mixed in with personal and family information.

Fill-in. Entry spaces generally are adequate. The professional field code entry, however, requires that the form be turned over to obtain the reference information. This is more time consuming than if the material were on the same side as the fill-in requirement.

The above forms are typical of forms used in soliciting responses from persons outside an organization. Poorly

EXHIBIT W
Biographical Data Form, *Who's Who in the East*

Who'sWho in the East 19th Edition 1983-1984

WE/DA
Biog. Ref

Biographical Data Form

PLEASE HELP US ASSURE ACCURATE, EFFICIENT HANDLING

- Please type or print clearly.
- Do not abbreviate.
- Please limit responses to information requested below.

U.S.A.

Name
Spell out names in full — First Name — Middle Name — Last Name

Professional Field Code ☐☐☐
Please see reverse side

Occupation
For example: Microbiologist, steel company executive, etc.

Place of birth

Date of birth
Add date of arrival and naturalization if applicable

Father's name
First — Middle — Last

Mother's name
First — Middle — Maiden surname (optional)

Education
Name of schools with dates of attendance, degrees received with dates, honorary degrees with names of school and dates.

Married
Complete maiden name of wife or husband's name

Date of Marriage
Month — Day — Year

Children
In order of birth

Brief career summary
Positions, firms, locations, and dates, in chronological order ending with current position.

Current position

Career-related activities
Corporate directorships or similar positions, teaching, consulting, etc.

Civic and political activities
Include offices held and dates

Military record
Dates and branch of service (active duty only)

Military decorations

Awards and certifications
Professional, public service, fellowships and grants.

SEE REVERSE SIDE

Do not attach to or write on this form anything other than the information requested.

designed forms sent out to obtain sales leads or for client processing may still achieve the desired result. If respondents are fundamentally interested in the product or service, they might complete the form no matter how confusing it is or how difficult the task.

In marginal cases, however, a good forms design could make the difference between the respondent completing or not completing the form. In these cases, the cost of improving a form may be more than compensated for by the increased volume of business generated.

An analysis of forms-improvement benefits can be readily accomplished in the use of promotional forms. Assessment of the value in a forms revision can be made by comparing the response volume and quality when using the revised form with that obtained when using the original form.

EXTERNAL PROCESSING AND OUTPUT

Business forms may be used to respond to inquiries, complaints, claims, orders, and the like. Forms that encourage quick and efficient response may often spell the difference between the continuing success and growth of a business or its decline and eventual failure.

A busy businessman may tell his secretary to clear off his desk. In the process, into the wastebasket may go inquiries and other valuable correspondence that the executive has piled up because there simply was not time to reply. This widespread practice of ignoring inquiries or delaying a response to correspondence has been found to be responsible for a large number of business failures (Elfenbein, 1972).

The average company takes from one to three weeks to answer inquiries, even from regular customers. Two of the chief reasons for failure to respond promptly are poor organization and the failure to develop an appropriately designed form to hasten the response.

Development of a forms-reply program involves the following steps:

1. Complete categorical analyses of all incoming correspondence
2. Identify the nature of the situations in the inquiry (sales order, product complaint, and the like)
3. Identify the events and response requirements indicated in the correspondence, such as request for product information and location of distributors, request for order-shipping date or to explain causes of delay
4. Prepare a preliminary draft of appropriate reply form
5. Test the form for use by appropriate department and staff
6. Evaluate quality of the form design against such criteria as:
   a. accuracy of response permitted in meeting information requirements of the correspondent
   b. staff acceptance of the form for routine use
   c. minimized visual discrimination and response time
   d. speed of overall response time

Exhibit X illustrates a standard reply form used by a customer-service department to handle inquiries, orders, and complaints. This form requires that the correspondence first be studied and the nature of the situation and event be determined. For example, a customer writes that an order was placed and not received after a reasonable period of time. The correspondent's file must be reviewed. The staff member using the form must scan it to see which items are applicable. Appropriate items are checked or filled in on the form and adjunctive material is attached if necessary. The form is addressed, dated, signed, and mailed to the correspondent.

This type of form provides for responses to a wide variety of situations, including shipping information, catalog requests, required remittance, return of materials, and requests for reply to earlier correspondence. The form,

EXHIBIT X

A form used to expedite replies to orders and inquiries.

TO ⌜ ⌝ DATE

⌞ ⌟

Dear Customer:

With reference to your order/letter/inquiry # __________ dated __________

we wish to inform you of the following:

1. Your order was shipped complete on __________ our invoice # __________.
2. Your order was shipped incomplete on __________ due to the fact that we were unable to ship the following title(s):

for the reason(s) checked below under # __________.

3. We are unable to make shipment because title(s) requested is/are
   a. ☐ Out of print.
   b. ☐ Temporarily out of stock. Title(s) has/have been back-ordered and will be supplied in approximately __________.
   c. ☐ Title(s) unclear. We are enclosing our catalogue and would appreciate your clarifying title(s) by return mail.
   d. ☐ Not our publication(s).
   e. ☐ New publication, still in production. We expect to supply in approximately __________.
   f. ☐ New publication. We are unable to inform you at this time when title will be ready. Should we cancel or hold your order until title is ready?
   g. ☐ Price incorrect; please confirm at correct price of $ __________.
   h. ☐ Title indefinitely out of stock. We are cancelling.
4. ☐ The title(s) listed under #14 below, ordered by you on the above order number/date is/are now available for immediate shipment. However, we would like to secure your confirmation of the above order in view of the delay that has occurred. You may signify your acceptance by simply returning this letter with the word "YES" written at the bottom.
5. ☐ We have been unable to locate your order. Please send us a duplicate copy of same.
6. ☐ Enclosed please find requested catalogue(s).
7. ☐ A remittance must accompany all orders, except when placed by authorized school personnel. Please add 10¢ per copy for postage and handling to the price of each book ordered.
8. ☐ Due to the fact that it is not our policy to ship C.O.D. orders, we would appreciate your favoring us with your remittance in the amount of $ __________ to cover the value of the book(s) requested. Your order will be processed as soon as your remittance is received. *Please return your order with check.*
9. ☐ Audio-visual or audio-lingual materials can only be sent on 30-day memo invoice. If material is returned within that time, invoice will be cancelled. Please reconfirm your request on this basis.
10. ☐ Imported titles can only be sent on 30-day memo invoice. If material is returned within this time, invoice will be cancelled. If class order of 10 copies or more of a title is sent, you may keep one copy of same title as a complimentary desk copy. Please reconfirm your request on this basis.
11. ☐ Permission is granted for return of clean, resalable stock. Please send merchandise prepaid, book post. Enclose this authorization and indicate our original invoice number.
12. ☐ Permission is granted for return of damaged or defective stock. Please send merchandise prepaid, book post. Enclose this authorization and indicate our original invoice number. Upon receipt of defective stock, replacement will be sent.
13. ☐ We are attaching copies of previous correspondence with you. Our files do not reflect having received an answer from you. Please answer our inquiry so that we can proceed accordingly.
14. ☐ Other reasons: __________

REPLY __________

DATE __________ SIGNED __________

Cordially yours,

Customer Service Department

however, is complex, requiring the staff respondent to make numerous discriminations and responses. This could increase the time it takes to answer the correspondence.

The form could be simplified for easier recognition of the content and more efficient completion, as shown in exhibit X-1. Considerable clerical time and effort are spent in reviewing the customer's file and determining status and background of the situation. However, improving design of the form can contribute to a reduction in response time. This, in turn, will also reduce the overall workload of the staff, further reducing delay or lag time when responding to correspondence.

INTERNAL PROCESSING AND CONTROL

Standard forms are used to expedite procedures within a business organization. Design of forms for internal use should be preceded by careful analysis of how current or projected internal procedures can be enhanced through the use of forms. The effective design and application of forms within an organization can result in major cost-saving benefits, which can be determined by the formula:

$$\frac{x - y}{x} \times 100 = \text{percent savings}$$

where x is a measure of time required to use the old forms procedure and y is a measure of time required to use an improved one. Further benefits can be realized by human-engineering refinements that reduce recognition, reading, and fill-in times while still yielding the essential information required.

A Form for Obtaining Credit Information

Exhibit Y presents a listing of credit information required by a credit department to expedite new customer orders.

EXHIBIT X-1

A simplified version of exhibit X.

Dear Customer:

This is in response to your order/letter/inquiry of ______________ 198__

1. Your shipment:

a. Was sent ☐ Invoice # ______________ Dated __________ 198__

b. Sent incomplete ☐ Dated __________ 198__ Titles missing __________

____

c. Not sent ☐ Reason:

Out of print ☐
Out of stock but on order ☐
Out of stock indefinitely ☐
Not our publication ☐
Title clarification needed ☐
Please clarify. See catalogue. ☐
Price correction needed ☐
Please correct. See catalogue. ☐

2. Your order:

a. Can now be filled ☐ Titles: ______________________

Please check if you still want these titles ☐ ______________

☐ ______________________________

☐ ______________________________

b. Was misplaced ☐ Please send us a copy.

3. Remittance required ☐ Please return this statement with payment of $____
Note: Individual orders must be prepaid.
C.O.D. orders not accepted.

4. 30-day memo invoice required ☐

Note: Audio-visual and audio-lingual materials, or imported titles can be returned within 30 days for cancellation. One desk copy of imported titles may be retained with orders of 10 or more.

Please indicate if this arrangement is acceptable.

5. Return the following ☐

Clean, resalable stock ☐
Damaged stock ☐

Note: Return prepaid book postage rate. Enclose this authorization, and indicate our original invoice number. Damaged stock will be replaced.

6. Please reply to our correspondence ☐ (Copy attached herewith).

7. Catalogue(s) enclosed ☐ Number of copies __________.

8. Other (as indicated) ☐ ______________________________

____

____

Cordially,

Customer Services

Each item requires a salesperson to use his or her own judgment about the depth of information to be included and to develop a detailed narrative credit report. This might consume a considerable amount of the salesperson's time without being especially cost effective, since much of the information included on the report may not be directly pertinent to establishing the customer's credit.

In the forms design process, the credit department should be carefully questioned to determine the most significant credit information items. Exhibit Y-1 presents a hypothetical forms design that reduces the salesperson's fill-in time while capturing most pertinent credit information. The form should be pretested on a group of salespeople to determine if the wording is clear and if changes are needed to secure essential, but not redundant, credit information.

Memo Forms

The way in which memo forms are designed can be important in developing efficient internal operations. Exhibit Z presents a universally used memo form that has been found to be only randomly effective. In fact, it may sometimes be a source of lost time and money. The message taker often fails to note the date and time, to include the phone number, to write out a clear message, and even to sign the memo.

The executive or business person with whom someone has tried to make contact would need to know the following in order to return the call:

1. Identity of caller (at least the last name and sex)
2. Time and date of contact
3. Firm the contact represents
4. Whether or not the call is urgent
5. How the contact was made—by phone or personal visit
6. The action that the caller would like the executive to take
7. Who completed the message form in case clarification is needed

EXHIBIT Y
An unstructured credit-information form.

Date ____________________

To: Our salesmen
From: Sales Manager
Subject: Credit Information

When you get an order from a new customer please fill out to the best of your ability the following report to assist our credit department and to assure prompt execution of the order.

1. Firm name: Is it a corporation, partnership, single owner?
2. Location: Exact address and zip code, physical size of store, type of neighborhood, competition?
3. How long in this location? Former location?
4. Full names and ages of owners, partners, officers.
5. Number of employees? Any relatives employed?
6. Principal type of merchandise carried.
7. Value and condition of inventory.
8. Value and condition of fixtures.
9. Layout orderly and clean?
10. Is stock insured against fire and theft?
11. Customer own or rent building? Amount of rental?
12. Is it a cash or credit business?
13. Store's record of expansion.
14. Sales volume over past four or five years.
15. Nature of owner's outside interests.
16. Owner's habits temperate?
17. Any present or financial difficulties?
18. Liability insurance?
19. Name of bank and branch
20. Number of trucks.
21. Local conditions.
22. Amount of local advertising.

Signature ______________________________

EXHIBIT Y-1
A redesigned credit-information form.

New Customer
Credit-Information Request
(Please Expedite)

1. Firm Name: ______________________ Type: Corporation ☐
Partnership ☐
Single Owner ☐

Street: ______________________

City: ______________ State: __________ Zip: ______

2. Names of Officers: ______________ Title: ________ Age: ______

______________ ________ ______

3. Bank: ______________ Branch Used: ______________

4. Approximate Size of Store:
- Less than 500 square feet ☐
- 501-1,000 ☐
- 1,000-2,000 ☐
- Over 2,000 ☐

5. Net property value:
- Less than $10,000 ☐
- $10,001-$20,000 ☐
- $20,001-$30,000 ☐
- Over $30,000 ☐

6. Number of employees:
- Less than 5 ☐
- 6 to 10 ☐
- 11 to 15 ☐
- 16 to 20 ☐
- Over 20 ☐

7. Store neighborhood:
- Lower income ☐
- Middle income ☐
- Upper income ☐

8. Years at present location:
- Less than 5 ☐
- 6 to 10 ☐
- Over 10 ☐

9. Location of nearest competitor:
- Within the same block ☐
- Several blocks away ☐
- About one mile away ☐

10. Principal merchandise:
- Dry goods ☐
- Hardware ☐
- Footwear ☐
- Headwear ☐
- Other (Describe) ☐

____

11. Value of merchandise:
- Less than $10,000 ☐
- $10,001-$20,000 ☐
- $20,001-$30,000 ☐
- Over $30,000 ☐

12. Is merchandise insured:
- Yes ☐
- No ☐

13. Annual advertising expenditure:
- Less than $5,000 ☐
- $5,001-$10,000 ☐
- $10,001-$15,000 ☐
- Over $15,000 ☐

14. Sales volume increase in the past five years:
- Less than $10,000 ☐
- $10,001-$20,000 ☐
- $20,001-$30,000 ☐
- Over $30,000 ☐

15. Owner's credit rating:
- Poor ☐
- Medium ☐
- Good ☐
- Excellent ☐

Signature: ______________________________________

EXHIBIT Z
The standard memo form used for recording contact messages.

To ______________________________

Date ____________________ Time ____________

WHILE YOU WERE OUT

M ______________________________

of ______________________________

Phone ______________________________

TELEPHONED		PLEASE CALL	
CALLED TO SEE YOU		WILL CALL AGAIN	
WANTS TO SEE YOU		URGENT	

Message ______________________________

____

____

____

____
Operator

A hypothetical redesign of the message form is presented in exhibit Z-1. This design provides more item structure than exhibit Z. Writing time is minimized by requiring only checking of appropriate boxes except for the contact's name, firm name and phone number, and date of contact. If other information must be included, an attachment could be used, or it could be written on the form itself. Names of the executives or business persons to whom the contact calls are made could also be printed on the form.

A color code could be employed to enhance item recognition, perhaps red for the "urgent" item. Pictorial coding for time might be used, as in exhibit Z-1.

In a trial comparision of the forms in exhibits Z and Z-1, fill-in time measures were obtained. A standard situation was used for comparison, such as one requiring that a phone call from a contact be returned. The actual measurement of fill-in time for the forms in exhibits Z and Z-1 were 66 and 44 seconds, respectively. The cost-saving formula:

$$\frac{66 - 44}{66} \times 100$$

would indicate a 33 percent saving in time. This could add up to a substantial saving in clerical time during the day. The revised form could simplify the message taker's task while providing more reliable information. However, there is still the possibility that information would be left out or errors made.

SUMMARY

Efficiency in the design and use of forms bears directly on the resource-management aspects of a business. Profitable use of forms may be made during three phases of a business operation: promotion and intake; external processing and output; and internal processing and control. Promotional and intake uses include forms designed to obtain marketing

EXHIBIT Z-1
A redesigned contact-message form.

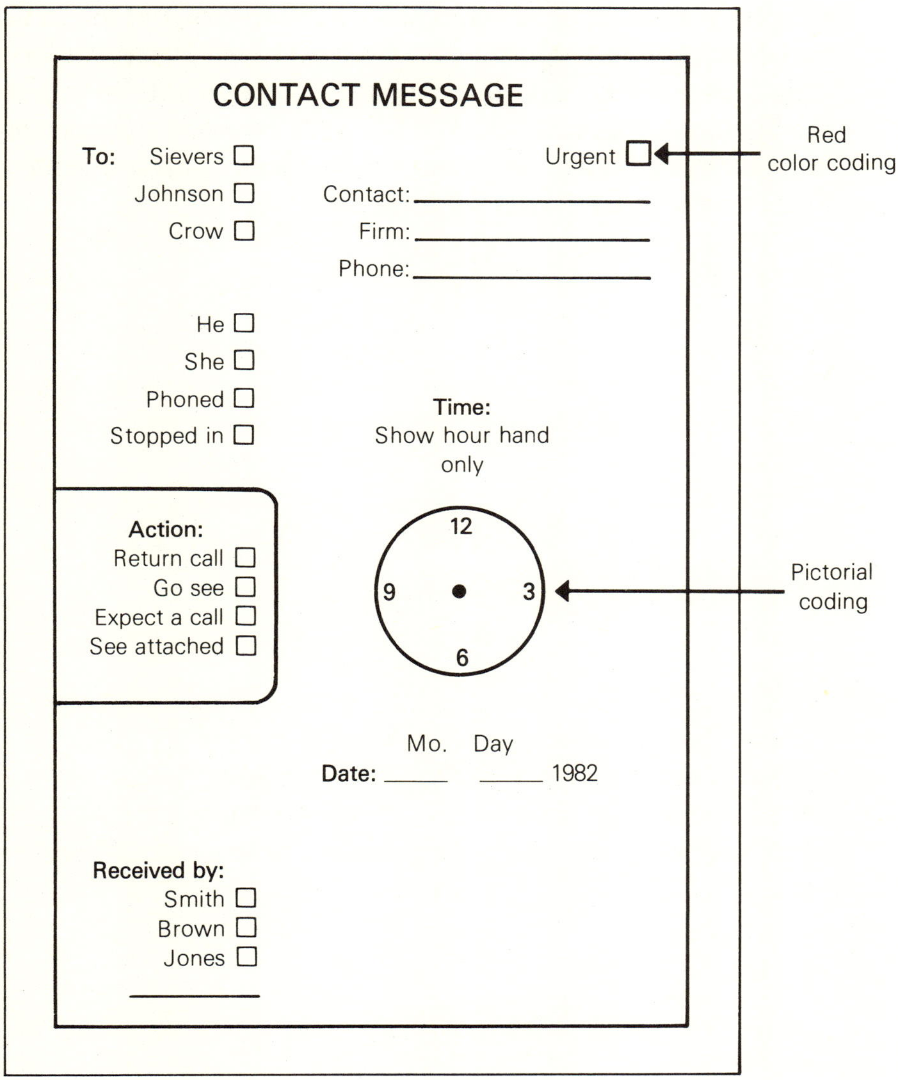

CONTACT MESSAGE

To: Sievers ☐ Johnson ☐ Crow ☐

Urgent ☐

Contact: ______

Firm: ______

Phone: ______

He ☐ She ☐ Phoned ☐ Stopped in ☐

Time:
Show hour hand only

Action:
Return call ☐
Go see ☐
Expect a call ☐
See attached ☐

Mo. Day
Date: ______ ______ 1982

Received by:
Smith ☐
Brown ☐
Jones ☐
______

survey data and to create sales leads and forms designed to provide efficient bank deposit and withdrawal procedures. External processing makes use of forms for quick and appropriate responses to inquiries, sales orders, complaints, and information requests. Internal processing and control uses forms to expedite the exchange of information within the business organization. The efficient application of forms to these three phases of operation is crucial to effective performance in the business enterprise.

CHAPTER 8

The Design of Engineering Information-Gathering Forms

Forms are used most extensively in government data processing and in routine business transactions. However, forms are also frequently used in the development of engineering data.

Engineering problems that may involve the use of forms include: (1) product improvement, (2) determination of incidents and conditions of unsafe operations, and (3) determination of user requirements to be incorporated into building-facility design. These problems require the engineer to develop data from the field, interrogating such consumers as product users, machine operators, accident victims and witnesses, and building occupants.

PRODUCT IMPROVEMENT INFORMATION

Consumer feedback provides an operational basis for engineering improvements. For example, the Smith-Corona typewriter cartridge ribbon system was designed in response to consumer input about the messiness of the inked ribbon on the spool, which had to be handled during ribbon change or readjustment. Given this information, engineers were able to design a system where handling or touching of the inked ribbon was avoided.

In product-engineering studies, where a large number of consumers can be questioned about their experiences with the product, the use of forms may be quite appropriate. (Appendix A shows typical questions employed in such investigations.) Investigations generating operational data for engineering improvements may involve direct observations, personal in-depth interviews, or the use of forms interrogating a representative sample of a user population.

Accident Investigations

To generate engineering improvements, injury investigations require that as much pertinent information be gathered as possible concerning causes of accidents. The investigator begins as far back in the history of the event as is practical, and asks not only what the worker was doing at the time of the injury, but what he or she was doing just before the accident. The investigator interviews the victims and witnesses to obtain as many pertinent facts as possible. He or she also closely examines the physical environment in which the injury occurred. The investigative techniques are largely personal interview and direct observation of the conditions or circumstances of the accident (Grimaldi and Simonds, 1975). Hence, the design and use of forms for such ad hoc events as accidents may be inappropriate unless a large number of victims or witnesses are involved.

Building-User Information

Functional-requirement statements on how a building will be used are essential design data upon which to base numerous facility development decisions (Dressel et al., 1977). The approaches taken for deriving facility-requirements information include the use of forms to interrogate building-user populations. In a military environment, for example, the question of whether a snack bar would be required in a facility was resolved through use of a questionnaire. Building occupants were asked about lunch and coffee breaks—whether they carried their lunch, went off base to civilian restaurants or bought snacks from a food vendor. They were asked how frequently they would use a snack bar. Such respondent data were used as criteria for deciding whether to include a snack bar in the facility. Similar questionnaires are given to service personnel for input that will help develop facility-design criteria for new processing centers, base commissaries, military dining facilities, and the like (Burgess, 1977).

THE PREPARATION OF ENGINEERING QUESTIONNAIRES

Engineers who prepare questionnaire forms may often be more oriented to the engineering aspects of design than to the user population from whom information is being sought. Engineers characteristically are quantitatively oriented. They think in terms of graphic plots and equations, which might be intimidating and confusing to the respondents who use products, machines, and facilities. Moreover, the engineers who design the forms may not have good verbal skills or the patience to write and rewrite the questions in order to improve readability and comprehension. Redundant questions may be improved as follows (Davis, 1963):

Poor	*Better*
Was an excessive quantity of acid present?	Was excess acid present?
Was the necessary work for proper preservation of the grinders done, which consists of cleaning, greasing and painting and any other work that is found necessary for the preservation of the grinders?	Were the grinders cleaned, greased, and painted for preservation?
In regard to replacements from some other manufacturer, were the supplies replaced by the original manufacturer due to sizes and design of their equipment?	Were supplies obtained from the equipment manufacturer?
What is the most common complaint you hear regarding processing procedures (not to be confused with the problems of the processee such as a housing shortage) like waiting in line or transportation around the post?	What is the most common routine processing problem?

A Critique of Engineering Forms Design

The engineer should orient his questions as efficiently as possible to the respondent population. If the questions are too general or too specific, information may be lost or incomplete, and user responses may be inappropriate to the engineering problem. In the U.S. Army Corps of Engineers, for example, a form has been developed for use by facility users to provide building space requirement information in accordance with Army Regulation 415-20, paragraph 5. The steps include the preparation of an outline for the project using flowcharts and the specification of what is required in the facility to perform necessary functions. The engineering form, to be completed either by current occupants or future facility users, is designated a "Project Development Brochure, Technical Manual 5-800-3." This requires respondents to list functions that will be carried out within the building, while stating what the associated equipment requirements will be.

Field personnel (master planners and facility engineers at individual bases) describe the form, which was developed by architectural engineers, as ineffective. Due to poor design of the new form, user requirements are often partially or wholly neglected. Major complaints of respondents include:

1. The required data development is too complex for a nontechnical user.
2. The information required is extensive and complicated, with no index provided for reference.
3. Clearer and more specific explanations are needed on how to fill out the forms.
4. Definitive statements are required, although users are often unable to state definitely what is needed in the facility.

5. The forms are too restrictive. They should serve only as a guide from which users can work up their own information.

The design of engineering forms thus may not provide enough guidance and direction on the one hand, while the forms themselves may be too restrictive in spelling out information requirements on the other.

Engineers may also fail to provide proper and consistent forms-completion instructions. They may ask for information that is not available to the respondent, while using technical terms that the latter cannot be expected to know. Even unavoidable technical terms may also go unexplained. The engineers, who by second nature respond to a problem quantitatively, may insist on graphs, flowcharts, mission and functions analysis, and other technical approaches that are beyond the respondent's technical capability. For example, a person who uses a ladder in different domestic applications may have no idea of such phrasing as stress factors, metal fatigue coefficients, or rung-spacing variables—but would know about such problems as carrying, placing, handling, adjusting, and working from a ladder. These are the areas of knowledge that an engineer should be concerned with when formulating questions for users.

Steps in the Development of Engineering Forms

The following procedures may be used by an engineer in designing a questionnaire:

1. Identify critical areas of product design
   a. prepare functional flowchart for processing the finished product
   b. specify design criteria
2. Identify personnel who can contribute to design solutions
   a. determine when and how the product is to be used
   b. determine personnel involved and the areas of their involvement

3. Block out areas in which questions are to be formulated
   a. define the operational phases of the product under investigation
   b. analyze information areas to be developed
   c. specify questionnaire items to be presented by functional areas of equipment operation, environmental and safety hazards, and potential human error
   d. index the questions on a section-by-section basis
   e. provide definitions and explanations where necessary
4. Prepare a pilot-interview form, test it on at least three representative users, and rework the questions and format as necessary
5. Obtain verifying data to confirm reliability of questionnaire data
6. Replicate the quesionnaire data on an additional user population and establish correlation

Identifying the Possible Problem Areas

Figure 8.1 presents a flowchart outlining phases that might be investigated in the design of a television set. Each block in the flowchart represents an area in which problems may occur. The persons responsible in each area may be designated as the users or respondents to whom questions can be directed. Installation problems, for example, might include assembly and placement of the set, antenna mounting, and connection and initial adjustment of control components. The respondents in this phase would be service and installation personnel.

In the operational phase, a general population of users of current model sets would be involved. Questions would encompass all aspects of set use—and viewing quality, convenience and effectiveness of controls, and overall reliability.

Some service and repair questions could be directed to the user population, such as malfunctions that require only simple adjustment. However, the bulk of questions in this

FIGURE 8.1
A flowchart covering the functional phases from design to use of a television set.

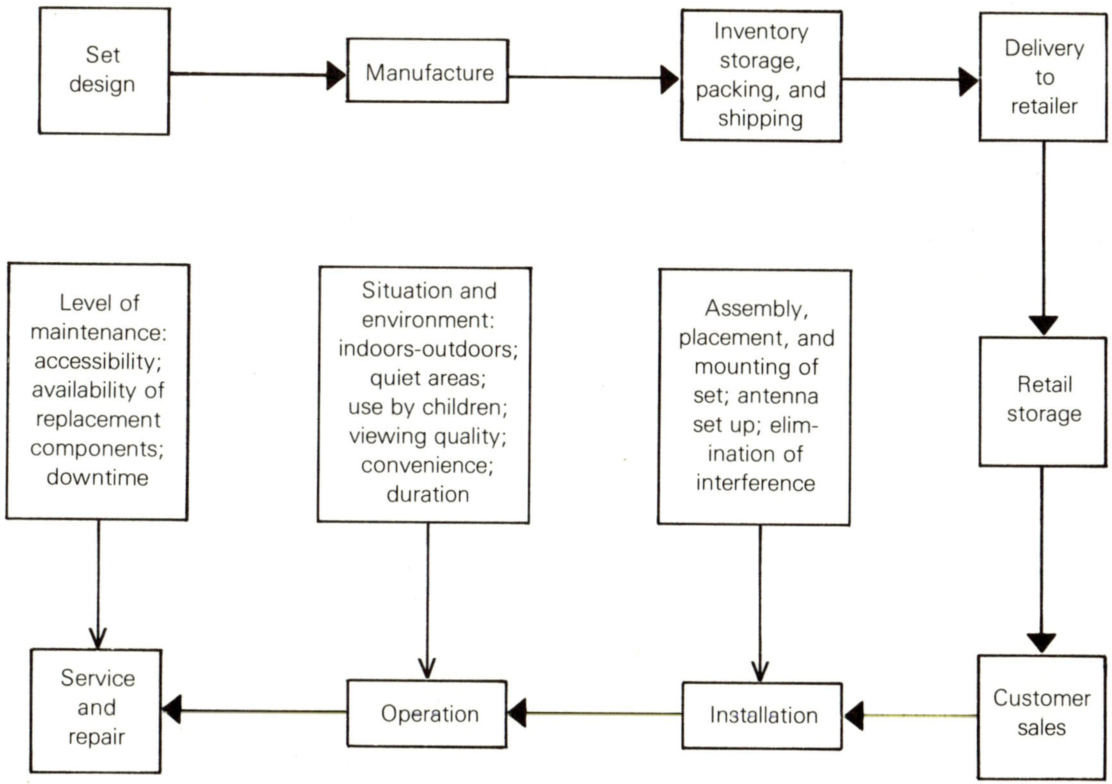

phase would concern operational performance and would, by and large, be directed to repair technicians.

Designing the Engineering Form

Engineering problems may involve one or more of the phases illustrated in figure 8.1. In each case, the problem-area questions must be asked as briefly as possible, while still yielding meaningful data that can be used for design improvements. Bear in mind that extensive and lengthy questionnaires are ignored by many consumers. However, if questions are brief and convenient to answer, and a self-addressed, stamped envelope is enclosed, returns should exceed 50 percent.

Exhibit AA presents a hypothetical form restricted to one problem area. The form requires only minutes to complete; hence, one could expect a relatively high rate of return. Through several different versions of the form, a wide variety of engineering questions could be addressed.

Piloting the Questionnaire

Before a questionnaire is distributed in quantity, a small group of respondents should test it. Two or three respondents would be sufficient, if they are representative of the respondent population and if their detailed responses are appropriately assessed. The initial draft of the form can then be revised, based on reactions and recommendations obtained in the pilot study.

Administering the Questionnaire

Standard statistical techniques can be employed using a population of thirty or more respondents. Samples of respondents should be drawn to be representative of the total population. Response reliability can be established through replication studies or by administering the questionnaire to a second sample of respondents.

EXHIBIT AA
An illustrative engineering questionnaire for television-set improvements.

Subject: Improving your Zopar Television

Dear Customer:

Our records indicate that you purchased a color Zopar television set a year ago. We are endeavoring to improve performance of the set. Would you please answer the following questions? A stamped return envelope is enclosed. Thank you.

Please check (✓) apropriate boxes below.

1. Does picture hold its sharpness?

yes ☐
no ☐

2. If no, when did it begin to fail?

After three months ☐
After six months ☐
After one year ☐

3. Which controls operate most poorly?

Remote channel selector ☐
Remote sound volume ☐
Color Tone ☐
Contrast ☐
Other (Describe) ☐

____

4. What tends to go wrong with the set most often?

Picture flops ☐
Image distorts ☐
Colors are not true ☐
Other (Describe) ☐

____

____

5. Your age?

Under 35 ☐
36 to 45 ☐
46 to 55 ☐
56 to 65 ☐
Over 65 ☐

6. Sex?

Male ☐
Female ☐

Follow-up

Experimental models, with a new design based on information derived from the questionnaire, should be specifically tested to assure that significant improvements have been made. For instance, if picture sharpness was found statistically in the questionnaire to fade after one year, tests should demonstrate that the new model holds its sharpness of image after, say, two thousand operating hours. Consumers who purchase the new model should be presented with the same questionnaire after owning the set one year. Engineering review might then indicate whether the new design has satisfactorily resolved the earlier engineering problem.

SUMMARY

Forms designed for engineering studies may concern product improvements, safety and injury investigations, or building-facility design. Product engineering and building-design studies may be most suitable for the use of questionnaire forms, since these generally involve large populations of users. In product-improvement studies, the questionnaires must be brief and convenient, or the user may refuse to respond. A wide range of engineering questions, however, can be addressed by presenting different questions on different forms and by using a large overall number of respondents. A product-improvement form development is outlined for a television set, and procedures are described to show how efficiently designed engineering forms can be developed.

CHAPTER 9
Processing and Using Forms-Derived Information

In the development of business forms, a forms administrator must work closely with the originators of the form, including those who will ultimately be using the information. Coordination by the forms-control staff begins with analysis of the need for the information. The procedure continues with deciding: (1) what specific information items will be included on the form; (2) how to arrange and format the form content; (3) how the quality can be controlled for efficient forms completion by respondents; (4) how the form can be efficiently processed; and (5) how the information can be effectively utilized for clerical or management tasks.

When business systems employed forms several decades ago, information was processed manually. Methods analysts were in control of the business operations. They were intimately aware of office routines and could help solve almost any procedural problem by working closely with concerned parties.

Modern technology has now made the old methods and systems generalists obsolete in all but the smallest of business organizations. The methods-and-procedures departments have evolved into computer analysis and programming groups. Forms information developments are largely intertwined with data processing. Modern forms developments must incorporate provisions for data input to the computer. Output of the computer is defined by computer programmers, who decide what formats will be developed. Thus, how forms-information will be processed and used is now thoroughly determined by computer-processing requirements.

FORMS INPUT TO COMPUTERS

Because forms are now commonly processed by computer systems, compromises are necessary between the mechanical needs of the computer process and the quality requirements for use by human respondents. When computer-system groups design forms they tend to orient them to the machine rather than to the respondent. Computer programmers may require special help to overcome this tendency. Close partnership must be arranged between the computer-systems group and the forms-design group in order to arrive at the best forms-design compromise.

The Computer Component

Computers, of course, operate on the basis of electrical impulses. The alphabetic and numerical characters that are read by the human respondent must be capable of being converted to electrical impulses.

The most common method of converting forms data to a form suitable for computer input is through keypunched cards. A conventional tab card consists of 80 vertical columns and 12 horizontal rows, for a possible total of 960 hole positions. A hole or combination of holes in one column represents one letter, number, or other character. A conventional keypunched card contains a maximum of 80 holes.

The cards are fed to a card reader where electrical impulses pass through the punched holes. These, according to their position, feed a specific letter, numeral, or character to the computer with each impulse. After the computer processes the data, the electrical impulses are converted back to letters, numerals, or characters. High speed printers are used to print out a computer paper message, or the message may be typed out on paper by a console typewriter, or it may be displayed on a cathode-ray-tube screen. The computer can also punch out tab cards, or it can provide audible messages using prerecorded words and sounds.

Input to the computer may also involve tapes or discs, with input typed in by an operator. A direct keyboard hookup to the computer can be used. Optical-character-recognition and magnetic-ink character-recognition readers are sometimes used where the computer can accept preprinted or even hand-printed data from a source document. The latter techniques are employed by banks, credit card operations, department stores, and so forth.

Programming the Computer

Programming begins with reviewing the needs of the information seeker. The programmers develop general, then specific, procedural flowcharts. Each step of the flowchart is written in a program language that the computer accepts. The coded program is keypunched on tab cards or otherwise converted to a form acceptable to a computer. After the initial testing of the program through computer runs, it is debugged, or corrected, and revised to make it ready for use in processing the forms data.

While the computer program processes the data input from the forms to yield meaningful summary information, this output process also presents artifacts of the program itself—the machine instructions. When these artifacts are carried on the printouts, the cluttered data may distract and confuse the person trying to read the substantive summary data. Further computer programs must then be written to suppress the artifacts from being printed in the printout.

Forms Used with Computers

Forms used for computer input are often called "source documents." Caution must be exercised in forms design to prepare source documents for easy conversion to a machine-processible form without sacrificing quality from the respondent's point of view.

An input operator transcribes fields and characters from the form onto keypunched tab cards, tapes, or discs. The operator works at a rapid pace and must be able to identify fields of information that are to be entered. Letters, numerals, and characters must be highly readable to facilitate speed and accuracy in transmission.

Input Fields. Usually only certain pieces of information are entered into a computer from the form. These are flagged for input by shading the group of items or outlining them with a heavy border. Shading may often reduce the visual contrast for both the respondent and the input operator. A variety of colors are used by different forms designers to shade the entry fields, and these are generally filled in by a respondent with a black or blue pen or pencil. If a standard color were adopted, a more effective design compromise might be possible. The field, for example, could be bright yellow, which yields excellent contrast with black or blue markings. Respondents who fill out forms generally recognize shaded or outlined fields as having to do with computers. However, the use of different colored fields on different forms may be distracting, not only because of poor contrast, but because the various colors may not be identified as computer related.

If standard yellow fields were adopted, not only would the necessary visual contrast be provided, but the color would be universally recognized as a field code that is used to bracket items for computer entry.

Input Characters. Separate boxes are generally provided on the form for each character to be entered into the computer, presumably to enable the input operator to read the character quickly and accurately. If not boxes, then small vertical lines are often used. However, studies show that writing one letter per box slows the writing and reduces legibility. The use of vertical lines results in even poorer performance for both writing and subsequent reading (Wright and Barnard, 1975). Simply providing blank lines to be filled in should simplify the task for both the respondent and the input operator.

Optical-Character-Recognition Readers. Scanning heads in the reader pick up whatever is not reflected back from a form. White paper reflects light back and is not read, whereas black ink does not reflect and is picked up by the scanning head. When marks or items are to be excluded from the computer, soft, faint colors are used. These will not be read by the scanning head. In the process, however, poor visual contrast is provided for the respondent. Readability for the respondent should be considered when employing a computer input technique.

FORMS-DATA UTILIZATION

Forms output data may be identified by their general operational uses, including: (1) ad hoc records, (2) recordkeeping with cyclical update or renewals, and (3) statistical or summary data for management information and decisions.

Ad hoc records are forms completed only once, such as shipping orders, birth certificates, marriage licenses, and personnel employment applications. These are usually filed away after they have served their purpose and are retrieved only to obtain information on the individual cases. A handwritten shipping order, for example, is sent to the warehouse for order filling, then to inventory control for posting to an inventory record. Copies are filed for reference.

Forms processed for cyclical updates are those requiring periodical processing, such as applications for vehicle and drivers' licenses, payroll records, or income tax forms. Generally, in these cases, summary data are not routinely required.

Management information derived from forms is primarily of interest as summary data. Summary data may be used to arrive at a number of management decisions, including corporate operations and financial adjustments, changes in product-line manufacturing, or new sales campaigns.

Forms used in business and government routines are fairly straightforward. Their utility can be readily assessed, with revisions and improvements incorporated on the basis of measurable time and efficiency factors. However, forms data developed for management-information purposes may be difficult to evaluate.

At a regional center of the Illinois Department of Mental Health, for example, a staff-activity reporting system was installed to derive management information. The system was costly, not only in the data processing per se, but in the staff time taken. Each staff member was required to spend from 5 to 10 percent of the workday completing the necessary forms. Moreover, the value of the reporting system was not assessed from a management-utility standpoint. Therefore, no accounting was made as to how frequently effective management decisions were made based on the data derived from the forms or whether the total regional mental-health policy benefited from the activity-reporting system.

Management-Information Data Systems

Forms data may be compiled for management to coordinate activities of various operational units and to develop efficiency in the operation as a whole. A sizable organization consists of multiple units requiring a communication network. Within the network there exists a hierarchy of decision-making functions, both within and among the units. Maintaining a structure for the efficient flow of information is essential to effective decision making (Deutsch, 1957). Criteria for making decisions are based on the optimizing of operations for the total organization. For example, an inventory system that maintains a full-storage status may not be best for the total organization. Such an inventory system is best understood and managed when viewed in perspective against the production, accounting, storage, and sales departments.

Management information is derived from assembling a number of data points in production time and costs, storage costs, and sales projections. The use of forms can supplement these hard data points with dynamic information on detailed operational and causal conditions about which various staff and department-level personnel are most knowledgeable. Forms information, however, must be carefully assessed for the effectiveness of its role in the decision-making process.

Use of Computer-Data Systems by Management

A survey of business executives across the country, conducted by the Dennison National Corporation of Holyoke, Massachusetts, indicated that computer-data systems are often counterproductive (*American Business,* 1982). Managers need to factor a wide range of economic and marketing data into their decisions. Yet computer data systems reportedly produce data that are too detailed and sometimes irrelevant to the management task.

Many computer operations have simply substituted for manual clerical functions, such as accounts receivable, payroll, billing, and invoicing. The management functions concern gathering information that affects decision making. Developing summary information for individual and group decision makers becomes a critical problem in formulating data items for respondents to complete or for selecting the data points most pertinent in management review. These are best determined through an iterative process or corrective feedback that must be based on a complete understanding of organizational dynamics (Mayers, 1970).

Computer processing of data often results in a type of data presentation that is unsuited to an executive's background, interests, and specific data needs. Computer printouts are generally cumbersome, carrying statements and artifacts of the computer program, its compiler, and its integrator. These often confuse and irritate the executive. Moreover, most executives are reluctant to use computers because they are not sufficiently familiar with them. An expensive terminal may sit in an executive's office unused for weeks at a time, so it becomes exorbitantly expensive because it is not used enough (Crawford, 1967). The Dennison survey indicated that computer manufacturers, programmers, and business administrators have a long way to go before management information will become significantly useful. The massive amounts of data spewed out by computers must be condensed and formatted so that the executive can use them effectively.

Current capabilities for presentation of data include graph displays from plotting devices, which are displayed on tape or oscilloscope screens. Output may also be presented as audio displays or computer-generated voice messages and written narrative reports produced by word processors. Prior determinations are not generally made as to what specific information an executive needs, nor have the methods of presentation been evaluated for effectiveness. This latter technology is only slowly beginning to develop (Nickerson et al., 1968; Parsons, 1970; Peace and Easterby, 1973; *Human Factors Society Bulletin,* 1977).

The Presentation of Summary Data

Though an abundance of data has been accumulated through forms, much of the information is not effectively employed by administrative managers. Joenk (1980) considers that information is usable only when it specifically addresses a given task or problem and when it is easily understood by managers who can appreciate its value. In order for a management-information service to develop usable information, it must understand the nature and purposes of persons using the information, their level of understanding, expectations, learning capabilities, and decision-making tasks. The information must be designed for comprehension, well organized and well presented, suitable to the task at hand, and easily readable.

Geiselman and Samet (1980) tested different approaches to the development and presentation of intelligence information for solution of military problems. Those participating in the study later were unanimously convinced that good summary information consists not only of hard facts, but also of an interpretation of the information. In this study, when a summary contained only a listing of facts, it was deemed to be a poor report whether the facts were categorized or not. Thus, information presented merely as factual was not understood as well as when the implications of the data were highlighted. For example, the statement "Respondents in the Eastern sector yielded a 30-percent higher interest response than those of the South or West" would be less meaningful than the summary statement "The introduction of the product throughout the New York-

Philadelphia area holds greater potential for success than it would if introduced in other parts of the country."

Samet and Geiselman (1981) formulated guidelines for the effective development of summary data as follows:

1. Prepare summaries in conversational form. Data listing alone makes understanding time consuming and difficult.
2. Give interpretation of the data when possible, that is, attempt to formulate conclusions based on the data when these can be well founded.
3. Include dynamic implications. For example, if respondents indicate a high level of interest in a product, show how interest level in the past has been correlated with later sales volume.

Visual Aids

The presentation of management information can also be markedly enhanced by the design of appropriate data displays. Quantitative data, for example, are best arranged in tabular form. Where trend information is required, a succession of data points or plotted graph data would likely be most effective. Discrete data such as a comparison of interest levels for two or three successive years may be best prepared with bar charts. When proportions or percentages are to be presented, pie charts could be used effectively.

Visual aids for use in preparing information summaries may require special design that is suitable to the specific purposes of a management operation. Scheduling decisions that must be made for lining up jobs on machines in a job shop, for example, are best implemented through the use of graphic presentations. A presentation method that listed machines by color code and time required for each job proved more effective than a conventional numerical listing of the jobs (Gibson and Lampros, 1978). Tullis (1981) found that graphic information on computer telephone lines that was displayed on CRT screens was not effectively improved through the use of color-graphic formats.

Universal methods for summarizing forms data cannot be recommended. Preparation of summary data and their visual displays should be tailored to the decision-making purposes for which the information was originally intended.

SUMMARY

In the development of forms, special consideration must be given to how the data will be processed and used. Modern forms-data processing methods involve the use of computers. Forms design must take into account both efficiency from the computer input-operator's standpoint and quality from the respondent's point of view.

Forms data are commonly used in computer processing in substituting for routine clerical functions such as registration procedures, accounting, payroll, billing, and inventory control. A more sophisticated use involves the development of management-information systems. In the past, management-information systems have proven to be inefficient and costly due to the lack of management experience with computers. An improved data-system design is necessary to provide management with more effectively usable forms-data summaries.

APPENDIX A
Sample Questionnaire Items

Following are examples of ways in which questions can be presented to respondents. Form items can be modeled in various structures: (1) selection of least to most; (2) ranking; (3) selection of correct or preferred area; (4) marking an agreement scale; (5) marking a semantic-differential scale. The effectiveness of each style of presentation can best be determined through empirical testing.

EXAMPLE 1. SELECTION OF LEAST TO MOST

In the following questions, make a mark along the line at a position best describing how you feel about the machine product you have purchased. For example, if you feel that it is more maintenance free than average, you would make a mark somewhere to the right of the center point, as illustrated here.

Highly unsatisfactory	Maintenance free ————————•————|——— CP	Highly satisfactory

Now complete each of the following in a similar fashion.

Highly unsatisfactory	Ease of control ————————•———————— CP	Highly satisfactory
Highly unsatisfactory	Operating noise ————————•———————— CP	Highly satisfactory

Note: This type of structure may employ a 100 millimeter line measured to the nearest tenth of a millimeter or numbered blocks that can be checked by a respondent.

EXAMPLE 2. RANKING

Read the list of machine improvements below and rank those that you consider to be the six most important. That is, next to number 1 place the letter of the improvement you consider most important, next to number 2 place the letter of the improvement you consider next most important, and so on, until all six are ranked.

a. Ease of maintenance	1	____
b. Better layout of controls	2	____
c. Better layout of displays	3	____
d. Reduced noise	4	____
e. Easier set-up provisions	4	____
f. Better instructions	6	____
g. Better lighting		
h. Damping out the vibrations		
i. Safety guards incorporated		
j. Reduced number of controls		
k. Other (Please describe):		

____

EXAMPLE 3. SELECTION OF A CORRECT OR PREFERRED AREA

How would you best recommend that the machine be changed to improve its operation? (Place an X in only one space below.)

1. Paint the outside surface to reduce glare ____
2. Combine the clutch and start operations ____
3. Insulate the motor to reduce noise ____
4. Provide safety plates around the gears ____
5. Other (Please describe): ____

   ____

   ____

EXAMPLE 4. MARKING AN AGREEMENT SCALE

Circle the numbers below which best represent your opinion.

	Strongly Agree	Agree	Neither	Disagree	Strongly Disagree
The machine has improved our operational performance and output.	1	2	3	4	5
The machine has an attractive and functional appearance.	1	2	3	4	5

EXAMPLE 5. MARKING A SEMANTIC-DIFFERENTIAL SCALE

Indicate how you would rate the machine environment by placing a check mark close to the adjective that best describes it. For example, if you feel that the area is extremely noisy, check close to the word "noisy" as shown below.

Noisy __ : ✓ : __ : __ : __ : __ : __ : __ : Quiet

Now complete the following in a similar fashion.

Chaotic __ : __ : __ : __ : __ : __ : __ : __ : Orderly
Dirty __ : __ : __ : __ : __ : __ : __ : __ : Clean
Dangerous __ : __ : __ : __ : __ : __ : __ : __ : Safe
Unattractive __ : __ : __ : __ : __ : __ : __ : __ : Attractive
Dark __ : __ : __ : __ : __ : __ : __ : __ : Light

APPENDIX B
An Evaluation Checklist for Forms-Design Critique

In evaluating a form under development or already in use, the following comprehensive human-factors design criteria should be applied. Each criterion is fully discussed in the text. An outline is provided here for quick reference in an evaluation review.

The evaluation can generally be completed through direct examination of the form and its fill-in instructions. However, items on information development (1-3) and development of fill-in instructions (48-49, 54, 58-60) should be evaluated by the forms designers.

FORMS INFORMATION ASSESSMENT

1. Were all possible alternatives to the use of a form considered? ____

2. Were the information items reduced to only those concerned with decision making and action? ____
3. Were the form items included on the basis of meaning to, and acceptance by, a representative sample of respondents? ____

ASSESSING FORMS CONTENT

4. Are only familiar words used? ____
5. Are only single-word or brief-sentence items used? ____
6. Is the active voice used? ____
7. Are negative words avoided? ____
8. Is the word "more" used rather than the word "less"? ____
9. Are only common abbreviations used, and then only when necessary? ____
10. Are specific references used without ambiguity? ____
11. Are all terms used consistently? ____
12. If sentences are necessary, are they brief, with no conjunctions and one verb only? ____
13. Are technical terms avoided? ____

EVALUATING FORMS CONFIGURATION AND LAYOUT

14. Is the form easy to identify by its general appearance? ____
15. Are headings and subheadings used to set the context? ____
16. Is coding used effectively in design:
    Color? ____
    Size? ____
    Shape? ____
    Location or space? ____
    Pictorial? ____

ASSESSING FORMS PRINT

17. Is black on white used for best contrast? ____
18. When colored printing is used, is color contrast provided? ____
19. Is red used against white or blue-green? ____
20. Is orange used against blue-green? ____
21. Is green, black, or blue used against bright yellow? ____
22. Are light blue and pale green avoided? ____
23. Is character height a minimum of one-twelfth of an inch? ____
24. Is the ratio of stroke width to character height about 1 to 8? ____
25. Is character width about 70 percent of the height? ____
26. Are characters unembellished? ____
27. Is upper- and lower-case lettering used? ____

ASSESSING FORMS ORGANIZATION

28. Are form items arranged in groups and subgroups? ____
29. Are items organized into logical groups? ____
30. Do the form sequences progress logically? ____
31. Are the sequences presented in the order in which they are to be completed? ____
32. Are the items easy to see as groups set off from each other? ____
33. Is clutter, or an excess of words and symbols, avoided? ____
34. Are sentences a maximum of three to five inches long? ____
35. Are headings printed perpendicularly at right angles to form items avoided? ____
36. Does printing always run horizontally rather than vertically? ____

37. Are all items numbered in sequence? ____
38. Is space optimally used, with minimum margin and item separation? ____

ASSESSING FILL-IN REQUIREMENTS

39. Are entry spaces adequate for maximum anticipated respondent response? ____
40. Are fill-in aids provided? ____
41. Does fill-in require excessive preparation or assembly of information? ____
42. Are the type of marks and writing instruments required for fill-in clearly indicated? ____
43. Are fill-in or entry spaces located to the right of or below each item? ____
44. Are fill-in spaces consistently located close to the item? ____
45. Are blank lines, rather than blocked-out spaces, provided for writing in information? ____
46. Are all words, numerals and symbols positioned at a normal reading angle? ____
47. Are necessary references located on the same side as the fill-in requirements? ____

ASSESSING FILL-IN INSTRUCTIONS

48. Are instructions based on a fill-in information requirements study? ____
49. Was the respondent population identified and studied? ____
50. Are only familiar words used? ____
51. Are idioms used? ____
52. Are relative pronouns used? ____
53. Are negatives used when such emphasis is required? ____

54. Were the instructions rewritten if necessary to improve clarity? ____
55. Are flowcharts used? ____
56. Are tabular formats used? ____
57. Are the print and paper used satisfactory:
    nonglossy paper? ____
    print of adequate size? ____
    colors of adequate contrast? ____
58. Is the reading level compatible with respondent reading competency? ____
59. Have reading-difficulty formulae been used in assessment? ____
60. Has conceptual comprehension been tested? ____

GLOSSARY

Ballot box

A small box aligned with a form item; the user selects an answer from among two or more alternatives.

Body

The main part of a form along with its title and instructions.

Business reply forms

Used for correspondence in order to speed up replies.

Cathode-ray tube

A television-type tube screen for displaying computer output; used with a keyboard to provide computer input.

CLOZE procedure

A technique to test comprehension in which every fifth word is left out and must be filled in by a respondent.

Coding

The use of different sizes, shapes, colors, and locations to set off or highlight items or parts of a form.

Completion aids

A forms-design element that helps a respondent complete the fill-in requirement, such as a partial date, a dollar sign, or colon.

Computer justification

Procedure establishing the value of a computer application in trade-off with manual (or other) processing means to analyze forms data, on the basis of such criteria as cost, accuracy, and speed.

Configuration reading

Form content grouped into visual patterns or arrangements to provide for easy and efficient checking of items.

Constraint

A requirement or limitation that must be met in forms design, e.g., reading level capability of a respondent population.

Content

The word difficulty, sentence structure, and phrasing to be used in a forms design.

Contingency question

An "if this, then this" type of form item. "If married, then how many children do you have?" is such a question.

Contrast

The difference in intensity between background and print elements.

Data massaging

Manual or computer processing of forms information to derive various statistical or actuarial measures.

Discrete display

A signal instrumented to indicate when an out-of-tolerance condition has occurred.

Engineering form

A question format presented to consumers or equipment operators to determine what design improvements might be made in a product.

Entry

A unit of information that is written on a form by a respondent.

Form face

The front side of a form.

Forms configuration

Visual grouping or patterns of items to facilitate recognition by a respondent or input operator.

Forms fields

Sections of a form shaded to show the input operator what information areas are to be entered into the computer.

Forms organization

The logical or illogical progression of forms content, and the order in which its items are presented.

Hard data

Variables taken from actual operational areas such as costs, frequency of complaints, number of manufacturing defects, or quality-control rejection rates.

Information requirement

A datum requirement or form item that can be demonstrated to fulfill a specific need in decision making or action taking.

Input operator

A person who converts computer programs and forms information to material that the computer will accept.

Internal-processing forms

Forms used to expedite procedures and operations within an office or shop.

Iteration

The process of review and correction.

Layout

Schematic drawing of a form showing the arrangement of items.

Literacy level

Reading and comprehension capabilities of a given population for whom forms or forms instructions are designed. Level might be established by standards tests.

Open-ended format

Phrasing of questions to permit individual, unstructured responses.

Optical scanner

A computer input device that reads letters, numbers, and characters, converting them to machine-usable codes.

Percentile

A statistical distribution divided into 100 parts of equal frequency.

Pilot study

A preliminary forms test in which a sample of typical users completes the form to determine design defects.

Point

Printer's basic unit of measure equal to approximately 1/72 inch.

Printout

A printed record produced as a computer output.

Programming artifacts

Statements in computer printouts that represent instructions the programmer has given the computer but that are irrelevant to the substantive information program.

Promotional forms

Forms used to develop sales leads in which potential customers answer questions relative to their need for, or interest in, a product or service.

Qualitative display

An indicator showing direction and magnitude of deviation from a standard.

Quantitative display

Readout yielding numerical values.

Readability formula

A reading-difficulty measurement that includes word difficulty (number of syllables) and sentence length.

Reader-oriented forms instructions

Instructions written and rewritten to improve their clarity specifically for respondent understanding.

Scanning head

The component of an optical reader, used for computer input, that picks up unreflected light.

Source document

The designation of a form when it is used for computer input.

Summary data

Processed forms information that is developed for use in decision making.

BIBLIOGRAPHY

Anisfeld, M. and I. Klenbort. "On the Function of Structural Paraphrase: The View from the Passive Voice." *Psychological Review* 1973, 79: 117-26.

Baker, C. and W. Grether. "Visual Presentation of Information." In *Human Engineering Guide to Equipment Design*, edited by C. Morgan et al. New York: McGraw-Hill, 1963.

Bendix, R. *Work and Authority in Industry*. New York: Wiley, 1957.

Benedon, W. *Records Management*. Englewood Cliffs, N.J.: Prentice-Hall, 1969. Chaps. 7 and 8.

Bennett, E. et al. *Human Factors in Technology*. New York: McGraw-Hill, 1963.

Berger, L. "Thoughts on the Semantics of Information." *ETC. A Review of General Semantics* 1971, 28: 421-25.

Biersner, R. and G. Bunde. "An Alternate of Performing Automated Readability Counts." *Human Factors Society Bulletin* 1979, 22: 1-3.

Blaiwes, A. "Formats for Presenting Procedural Instructions." *Journal of Applied Psychology* 1974, 59: 683-86.

Blumenthal, A. "Observations with Self Imbedded Sentences." *Psychonomic Science* 1966, 6: 453-54.

Brandsford, J. and J. Franks. "The Abstraction of Linguistic Ideas." *Cognitive Psychology* 1971, 2: 331-50.

Brown, R. "The Development of Questions in Child Speech." *Journal of Verbal Learning and Verbal Behavior* 1968, 7: 279-90.

Burgess, J. "Ego Involvement in the Systems Design Process." *Human Factors* 1970, 12: 1-12.

Burgess, J. "Enlisted Personnel Dining Facility Modernization Evaluation Program." Champaign, Ill., Department of Army, Construction Engineering Research Laboratory, 1977, Report D-77.

Burgess, J. *Systems Design Approaches to Public Services.* Cranbury, N.J.: Associated University Presses, 1978.

Chapanis, A. "Words, Words, Words." *Human Factors* 1965, 7: 1-17.

Chapanis, A. "Human Factors Systems Engineering." (Chapter 2) In *Systems Psychology*, edited by K. DeGreene. New York: McGraw-Hill, 1970, pp. 54-56.

Cherry, C. *On Human Communication.* New York: Wiley, 1961.

Christ, R. "Review and Analysis of Color Coding Research for Visual Displays." *Human Factors* 1975, 17: 542-70.

Clark, H. and W. Chase. "On the Process of Comparing Sentences Against Pictures." *Cognitive Psychology* 1972, 3: 472-517.

Clark, H. and E. Clark. "Semantic Distinction and Memory for Complex Sentences." *Quarterly Journal of Experimental Psychology* 1968, 21: 137-47.

Clark, L. "Records Management." In *Business Systems.* Cleveland, Ohio: Association for Systems Management, 1970. Chap. 8.

Coleman, E. and S. Hahn. "Failure to Improve Readability with a Vertical Typography." *Journal of Applied Psychology* 1966, 50: 434-36.

"Computer Is No Match for Execs." *American Business*, Feb. 1982, p. 10.

Conrad, N. and A. Hull. "Copying Alpha and Numeric Codes by Hand." *Journal of Applied Psychology* 1967, 51: 444-48.

Crawford, A. "On Identifying Critical Elements of Industrial Information Systems." In *The Human Operator in Complex Systems*, edited by W. Singleton et al. London: Taylor and Francis, 1967, pp. 139-50.

Curry, R. et al. "A Design Procedure for Control/Display Systems." *Human Factors* 1977, 19: 421-36.

Davis, D. *Elements of Engineering Reports.* New York: Chemical Pub. Co., 1963.

Davis, G. *Introduction to Electronic Computers.* New York: McGraw-Hill, 1965.

DeGreene, K. *Systems Psychology.* New York: McGraw-Hill, 1970.

DeGreene, K. *Sociotechnical Systems. Factors in Analysis, Design and Management.* Englewood Cliffs, N.J.: Prentice-Hall, 1973.

Deutsch, K. "On Communication Models in Social Science." *Public Opinion Quarterly*, 1957, pp. 356-80.

Dooling, D. and R. Lachman. "Effects of Comprehension on Retention of Prose." *Journal of Experimental Psychology* 1971, 88: 216-22.

Dressel, D., et al. "Improvement to Procedures for Deriving Functional Requirements from Organizations and Individuals." Champaign, Ill., Department of Army, Construction Engineering Research Laboratory, 1977, Report D-80.

Drury, C. and M. Clement. "The Effect of Area, Density, and Number of Background Characters on Visual Search." *Human Factors* 1978, 20: 597-602.

Dyer, F. and J. Dyer. *Bureaucracy vs. Creativity.* Coral Gables, Fla.: University of Miami Press, 1969.

Eale, E. and J. Chall. "A Formula for Predicting Readability Instructions." *Education Research Bulletin,* Feb. 18, 1948.

Elfenbein, J. *Handbook of Business Form Letters and Forms.* New York: Simon and Schuster, 1972.

Flesch, R. "A New Readability Yardstick." *Journal of Applied Psychology* 1948, 32: 221-33.

Gade, P. et al. "Data Entry Performance as a Function of Method and Instruction Strategy." *Human Factors* 1981, 23: 199-210.

Gamble, L. and P. Kincaid. "New Easy-to-Read Insurance Policies: How Easy Are They to Understand?" *Human Factors Society Bulletin* 1976, 19: 4-5.

Geiselman, R. and M. Samet. "Summary Military Information. An Application of Schema Theory." *Human Factors* 1980, 22: 693-705.

General Services Administration. *Records Management Handbook and Forms Management.* Washington, D.C.: National Archives and Records Management, n.d.

Gibson, R. and L. Lampros. "The Presentation of Information to the Job Shop Scheduler." *Human Factors* 1978, 20: 725-32.

Goldman-Eisler, F. and M. Cohen. "N, P, and PN Difficulty: A Voted Criterion of Transformational Operation." *Journal of Verbal Learning and Verbal Behavior* 1970, 9: 161-66.

Gran, M. "Questionnaire Typology and Production." *Applied Ergonomics* 1975, 6: 81-89.

Green, P. and R. Pew. "Evaluating Pictographic Symbols. An Automotive Application." *Human Factors* 1978, 20: 103-14.

Greene, J. "The Semantic Function of Negatives and Passives." *British Journal of Psychology* 1970, 16:17-22.

Grimaldi, J. and R. Simonds. *Safety Management.* Homewood, Ill.: Irwin, 1975.

Hakes, D. and D. Foss. "Decision Processes During Sentence Comprehension: Effects of Surface Structure Reconsidered." *Perception and Psychophysics* 1970, 8: 413-16.

Hammer, C. and S. Ringel. "Information and Assimilation from Coded and Uncoded Individual and Grouped Displays." *Human Factors* 1965, 7: 245-55.

Haney, R. "The Effect of Format on Functional Testing Performance." *Human Factors* 1969, 12: 181-88.

Hodges, J. and B. Angalet. "The Primary Technical Information Source —The Local Work Environment." *Human Factors* 1968, 10: 425-30.

"Human Factors and Computers." *Human Factors Society Bulletin,* 1977, 20: 8-9.

"Intelligible Tax Forms Are Tested." *Moneysworth,* March 1982, p. 16.

Joenk, R. "Special IEEE Issue: Making Information Usable." *Human Factors Society Bulletin* 1980, 23: 7.

Johnson, D. and H. Altman. "Effects of Briefing Card Information on Passenger Behavior during Aircraft Evacuation Demonstrations." In *Proceedings of the Seventeenth Annual Meeting of the Human Factors Society.* Santa Monica, Calif.: The Human Factors Society, 1973.

Kammann, P. "The Comprehensibility of Printed Instructions and the Flow Chart Alternative." *Human Factors* 1975, 17: 183-91.

Katz, D. and R. Kahn. *The Social Psychology of Organizations.* New York: Wiley, 1966.

Kilty, T. "The Readability of Commonly Encountered Materials." *Human Factors Society Bulletin* 1976, 19: 3-4.

Kincaid, J. and L. Delionback. "Validation of the Automated Readability Index: A Followup." *Human Factors* 1973, 15: 17-28.

Kish, J. *Business Forms Design and Control.* New York: Ronald Press, 1971.

Klare, G. "Assessing Readability." *Reading Research Quarterly* 1974, 10: 62-102.

Klare, G. et al. "The Relationship of Verbal Communication Variables to Immediate and Delayed Retention and to Acceptability of Technical Training Materials." Chanute Air Force Base, Rantoul, Ill., U.S. Air Force Training Aids Research Laboratories, 1954, Report AFPTRC, 1954, pp. 54-103.

Klare, G., et al. "The Relationship of Pattern (Underlining) to Immediate Retention and to Acceptability of Technical Materials." *Journal of Applied Psychology* 1955, 39: 40-42.

Knox, F. *Design and Control of Business Forms*. New York: McGraw-Hill, 1965.

Kolers, P. "Reading Temporally and Spatially Transformed Text." In *The Psycholinguistic Nature of the Reading Process*, edited by K. Goodman. Detroit, Mich.: Wayne State University Press, 1968.

Kolers, P. et al. "Eye Movement Measurement of Readability of CRT Displays." *Human Factors* 1981, 23: 517-27.

Kolers, P. et al., eds. *Processing of Visible Language*. New York: Plenum Press, 1980.

Levine, J. "Information Seeking with Conflicting and Irrelevant Input." *Journal of Applied Psychology* 1973, 57: 74-80.

Levine, J. et al. "Information Seeking and Limitation on Available Information and Resources." *Human Factors* 1975, 17: 502-15.

Lintz, P. "Using Familiar Words in Technical Writing." *Human Factors Society Bulletin* 1979, 22: 5-7.

Loftus, E. et al. "Retrieval of Words from Subordinates and Superordinate Categories in Semantic Hierarchies." *Psychonomic Science* 1970, 21: 235-36.

Lurie, W. "The Impertinent Questioner." *ETC. A Review of General Semantics* 1962, 19: 94-100.

Mahoney, T. "Weighted Application Blank Analysis of Contingency Items." *Journal of Applied Psychology* 1958, 42: 60-62.

Marien, R. *Marien on Forms Control*. New York: McGraw-Hill, 1965.

Mayer, S. "Trends in Human Factors Research for Military Information Systems." *Human Factors* 1970, 12: 177-86.

McCormick, E. "Human Factors in Systems Development." In *Human Factors Engineering*. New York: McGraw-Hill, 1970, pp. 17-50.

McKendry, J. and T. Enderwick. "Judgmentally Derived Information Utility Estimates." In *The Human Operator in Complex Systems*, edited by W. Singleton et al. London: Taylor and Francis, 1967, pp. 87-94.

Melby, M. et al. "Written Communication: A Systems Approach. *Human Factors Society Bulletin* 1977, 20: 1-3.

Morey, N., ed. *Mental Workload: Its Theory and Measurement.* New York: Plenum Press, 1979.

Nickerson, R. et al. "Human Factors in the Design of Time-Sharing Computer Systems." *Human Factors* 1968, 10: 127-34.

Norcott, N. *Adult Functional Competency: A Summary.* Washington, D.C.: U.S. Office of Education, 1975.

Noyes, L. "The Positioning of Type on Maps: The Effect of Surrounding Material on Word Recognition." *Human Factors* 1980, 22: 353-60.

Nygren, W. *Business Forms Management.* New York: AMACON, Division of American Management Association, 1980.

Olson, D. "Language and Thought Aspects of a Cognitive Theory of Semantics." *Psychological Review* 1970, 77: 257-73.

Osgood, C. et al. *The Measurement of Meaning.* Urbana, Ill.: University of Illinois Press, 1957.

Palermo, D. "More About Less: A Study of Comprehension." *Journal of Verbal Learning and Verbal Behavior* 1973, 12: 211-21.

Parsons, H. "The Scope of Human Factors in Computer Based Data Processing Systems." *Human Factors* 1970, 12: 165-75.

Parsons, S. "Signs of the Times." *Human Factors Society Bulletin* 1979, 22: 3.

Peace, D. and R. Easterby. "The Evaluation of User Interaction with Computer Based Management Systems." *Human Factors* 1973, 15: 163-77.

Peterson, D. and M. Tinker. "Studies of Typographical Factors Influencing Speed of Reading Black Type Versus White Type." *Journal of Applied Psychology* 1931, 15: 241-47.

"Physicians' Handwriting and Wasted Time." *Journal of the American Medical Association* 1979, 42: 2429-30.

Poulton, E. "Rate of Comprehension of an Existing Teleprinter Output and Possible Alternatives." *Journal of Applied Psychology* 1968, 52: 16-21.

Poulton, E. "Skimming Lists of Food Ingredients Printed in Different Brightness Contrasts." *Journal of Applied Psychology* 1969, 53: 55-58.

Samet, M. and R. Geiselman. "Developing Guidelines for Summarizing Information." *Human Factors* 1981, 23: 727-36.

Senensieb, N. "Corporate Systems and Procedures." In *The Information Systems Handbook,* edited by F. McGarlan and R. Nolan. Homewood, Ill.: Irwin, 1975.

Shontz, W. et al. "Color Coding for Information Location." *Human Factors* 1971, 13: 237-46.

"Simplified Style Proposed for Business Letter Writing." *Human Factors Society Bulletin* 1981, 24:4.

Smith, E. and J. Kincaid. "Derivation and Validity of the Automated Readability Index for Use with Technical Material." *Human Factors* 1970, 12: 457-64.

Smith, S. "Letter Size and Legibility." *Human Factors* 1979, 21: 661-70.

Smith, S. "Exploring Compatibility with Words and Pictures." *Human Factors* 1981, 23: 305-15.

Solomon, R. and L. Postman. "Frequency of Usage as a Determinant of Recognition Threshold for Words." *Journal of Experimental Psychology* 1952, 43: 195-201.

Stamper, R. *Information in Business and Administration Systems.* New York: Halsted Press, 1975.

Stanlee, L. and N. Fattu. "Readability of Navy Publications." *Journal of Educational Research* 1956, 49: 471-73.

Strauss, E. *The Ruling Servant.* London: George Allen and Unwin, 1961.

Tichy, H. *Effective Writing for Engineers, Managers, Scientists.* New York: Wiley, 1966.

Tinker, M. *Legibility of Print.* Ames: Iowa State University Press, 1964.

Tinker, M. *Bases for Effective Reading.* Minneapolis, Minn. University of Minnesota Press, 1965.

Trabasso, T. et al. "Storage and Unfamiliar States in Processing Concepts." *Cognitive Psychology* 1971, 2: 239-89.

Tullis, T. "An Evaluation of Alphanumeric, Graphic and Color Information Display." *Human Factors* 1981, 23: 541-50.

VanCott, H. and J. Altman. "Procedures for Including Human Engineering Factors in the Development of Weapon Systems." Wright Air Development Center, Dayton, Ohio, WADC TR 56-488, 1956.

Van Nes, F. and H. Bouma. "On the Legibility of Segmented Numerals." *Human Factors* 1980, 22: 463-74.

Wason, P. "Response to Affirmative and Negative Binary Statements." *British Journal of Psychology* 1961, 52: 133-42.

Weber, M. *The Theory of Social and Economic Organization,* translated by A. Henderson and T. Parsons. New York: Oxford University Press, 1947.

Wiedman, T. and F. Ireland. "A New Look at Procedures Manuals." *Human Factors* 1965, 7: 371-77.

Williams, C. "Horizontal Versus Vertical Display of Numbers." *Human Factors* 1966, 8: 237-38.

Wright, P. "Transformations and the Understanding of Sentences." *Language and Speech* 1969, 12: 156-66.

Wright, P. and P. Barnard. "Just Fill in This Form—A Review for Designers." *Applied Ergonomics* 1975, 6: 213-20.

Wright, P. and F. Reid. "Written Information: Some Alternatives to Prose for Expressing the Outcome of Complex Contingencies." *Journal of Applied Psychology* 1973, 57: 160-66.

INDEX

Accident investigations, 140
Active voice, 22, 26, 71
Ad hoc records form, 155–56
Adjectival modifiers, 24
Affirmative statements, 22, 54
Ambiguities, avoiding, 23
Automobile-insurance-sales-leads form, 112, 114
Automobile-registration form, 102–3

Ballot-box entries, 41, 77, 79, 112, 155
Bank deposit and withdrawal forms, 121–22
Bar charts, 160
Blank-line entries, 41, 155
Boxes, fill-in. *See* Ballot-box entries
Building-facility design forms, 139, 141, 149; and building-user interrogation, 141, 143–44
Bureaucracies, 1, 65–69, 90, 106; hierarchies in, 66; insistence on efficiency in, 69, 106; internal interdependencies in, 66; mission of, 106; structure and operation of, 69
Business, 9, 27, 31; success formula, 109
Business-form design, 109–38, 139, 151

Captions and legends, 41
Car registration, 1
Characters per line, 61
Character style, 33, 34
Clarity of information, 5
Clauses, 53
Clerical functions, 158; costs of, 6
"Cloze" procedure, 62
Clutter, 37, 86, 93, 154
Coding, 29, 30, 41; color, 29, 30, 41; geometric, 37; group, 31, 36, 37; pictorial, 29, 31, 37, 111; recognition value of, 30; separation, 37; shape, 29, 31; size, 29, 31; space, 29, 31
Completion aids, 44

Completion time, 29, 44
Complex sentences, 53, 76, 77, 81, 111, 123
Compound questions, 24
Comprehension, 25, 36, 76, 86, 90, 142
Computer analysis and programming, 152
Computer artifacts, 154, 158
Computer components, 152–55; input characters, 155; input fields, 154–55; optical readers, 155
Computer data systems, 157
Computer input, 153
Computer-input operator, 154
Computer processing, 40, 44, 98, 153; printout in, 8, 153
Computer programmers, 152
Computer system groups, 152
Conceptual difficulty measurement, 62
Configurational arrangement, 37
Conjunctions and disjunctions, 24
Consecutive item numbering, 117, 119
Constraints on forms, 5, 6, 30
Consumers, 147
Contact form, 132, 137
Content design, 29
Corrective action, 35
Cost accounting, 5, 7, 8, 156
Cost effectiveness, 8, 19, 132, 158
Cost(ing), 8, 48, 127
Cost-saving, 66; benefits of, 130; formula for, 130
Cost vs. value, 18–19
Customer complaint analysis, 14, 41–44
Customer-complaint form, 35, 41–44
Customer relations, 11, 13, 14–17
Customer response, 110
Customer-service department, 128
Customer services, 16
Credit-information form, 130, 133, 134
Critical areas on forms, 30
Cyclical records form, 155–56

Dale-Chall readability formula, 61
Data entry, 4, 5
Data gathering, 4
Data items, 9
Data loss, 23
Data points, 157, 158
Data presentation, 158–61
Data summary, 2
Decision-based action, 12, 18
Decision makers, 10, 157–61
Decision-making process, 157
Design improvements, 147
Display reading, 28
Double spacing, 59
Driver registration form, 99–101

Elderly respondents, 33, 39, 76, 81, 86–89, 92, 93, 112, 119–21
Electronic data processing, 9, 33, 152–54
Electronic reader, 33, 153
Embellished characters, 34, 35. *See also* Printing
Empirical evaluation, 38
Encoding, 5, 6

Engineering forms, 31, 139–50; critique of, 143; followup, 149; steps in formulating, 144–49
Engineering questionnaires, 141–42, 144
Engineers, 32, 141
Entrepreneurs, 65, 66
Entry spaces, 44. *See also* Fill-in
Error, 6
Evaluation, 4, 90, 127, 128, 136
Executive(s), 6, 132, 136, 157, 158
External-processing-and-output forms, 110, 127–30

Feedback loop, 11, 12
Fill-in, 27, 28, 30, 37–38, 39, 40; aids, 40, 117; error, 8, 37; spaces, 40, 77; time, 41, 45, 77
Fill-in instructions, 47–64, 170; conceptual evaluation of, 63; direct and uncomplicated, 47–48; empirical assessment of, 62; rational assessment of, 61
Flesch Reading Ease Score (FRES), 62
Flowcharts, 56–57, 143, 153
Formats, 5, 6, 8, 24, 44, 55, 56–57, 158; open-ended, 18, 111
Form(s): abbreviations in, 115; administration of, 38, 151; alternative, 2–3, 4; caveat(s), 121; circulation of, 28, 39; coding in, 76, 77, 80, 81, 87, 92, 98, 115, 117, 119, 121, 136; completion of, 4, 5, 7, 28, 39; complexity of, 130; computer processed, 98, 99, 151–62; configuration of, 76, 77, 80, 81, 87, 93, 111, 115, 117, 119, 121, 123, 125, 168; content of, 6, 14, 26, 36, 77, 81, 86, 87, 93, 98, 111, 112, 115, 117, 119, 121, 123, 125, 151, 168; contrast in, 80, 81, 93, 99, 123, 154, 155; control group, 10, 11, 12, 13, 151; and cost-savings, 130, 136; design compromise, 152; design criteria, 6, 28, 152; design of, 2, 4–5, 21, 23, 24, 31, 48–49, 50; development of, 18; evaluation of, 2–3, 65–107, 109–38; fill-in, 7, 76, 77, 81, 86, 87, 93, 98, 104, 112, 115, 117, 119, 121, 123, 125, 128, 130; headings on, 86, 115, 117, 121, 123; improvement of, 66, 71, 106, 127, 130, 131, 132, 137; innovative changes in, 65; input, 38–41; instructions on, 40; inventory, 2; items on, 2, 48; layout of, 5, 39, 41–44, 145, 168; order, 11; organization of, 35–38, 76–77, 78, 81, 86, 87, 93, 98, 104, 112, 115, 117, 119, 121, 123, 125, 169; originator of, 27; pretesting, 132, 147; printing, 2, 76, 77, 81, 93, 98, 104, 112, 115, 117, 119, 121, 123, 125, 169; processing, 2, 4, 38, 151; quality, 110, 128, 151; readability of, 32–35; recognition of content in, 88; request, 2, 10; review, 48–49; scanning, 28; security, 7; simplification of, 130; space saving, 87;

transmission of, 5; used for correspondence, 127–30; used for internal-processing control, 130–37; used for processing correspondence, 110; uses of, 7; voice in, 92–93, 119
Forms-reply program, 128
Form 1040, 71–77
Form 1040A, 77–78
Form 1040S, 90
Form 1040 Schedules A and B, 80, 82–83
Form 1040 Schedule E, 81–84, 85
Form 1040 Schedules R and RP, 86–89
For-office-use-only explanations, 119
FRES. *See* Flesch Reading Ease Score
Functional areas, 13, 145–46
Functions listing, 143

General Services Administration, 70
General-to-specific sequencing, 35
Geometric shapes, 31. *See also* Coding
Goal(s), 3, 12, 13, 17, 27, 104; definition of, 11, 13; quantified, 13–14
Government forms, 9, 27, 65–107; for agencies, 95; and data, 139; design and evaluation of, 70; operational differences with private business, 66–68; strategies for improvement in, 66, 106
Graphic information, 160
Grouping, 37

Hard data, 14, 157
Headings, 29, 41, 45, 86, 98
High-speed printers, 153
Human engineering, 21, 27–28, 45; design standards, 29
Human-factors analysis, 2; and design criteria, 5; principles of, 2, 41, 71

Idioms, 51, 52
Ignoring inquiries, and business success, 127
Imperative mood, 53
Income tax, 1
Information element, 28
Information feedback, 29
Information issues, 17–19
Information item analysis, 16, 18, 21
Information item specification, 17
Information-requirements analysis, 5–6, 8, 9–19, 21, 132, 151; discrete data, 6; goals of, 11; quantitative data, 6; rationale for, 11
Information value, 10, 11, 156, 159
Initiating group, 11, 12, 17–18, 27
Input, 29. *See also* Fill-in
Instructional aids, 4–5
Instruction(s), 6; designing, 55–61; evaluation and review of, 61, testing, 59
Instructions writer, 51
Internal processing forms, 110
Interpretability, 30
Interpretational variables, 48
Interrelated meanings, 53
Irrelevant items, 18

I.R.S. forms, 70–90; improvement program for, 70, 90; instructions, 55–56; tabular format, 59; and tax laws, 71
Item structure, 24–25

Journal-soliciting form, 119–20

Keypunch, 7
Keypunched cards, 152–53

Label(s), 76, 77
Layout plane, 36–37
"Less-than" items, 86
Lighting, 35
Locating time, 41
Logical sequences, 35, 42–44, 45, 76, 80, 81, 86, 99
Low-yield items, 18, 19

Machine processing, 8
Management, 6, 13
Management information, value of, 159
Management-information forms data, 156, 157, 161
Management summary data, 159–61; guidelines for, 160; prepared interpretations of, 159; visual aids for presenting, 160
Manpower requirements, 19
Marking, 40; space, 38, 39
Memo form, 132, 135, 137
Methods analysts, 151
Michigan Social Service application forms, 61
Millilambert, 35
Mood and voice, 53–54
Multiple-conditions response, 114–15

Narrative instruction, 59
National Health Insurance application, 61
Negative emphasis, 54, 99, 104, 125
Negative words, 22–23, 54, 76, 80, 93, 117, 123
New York State Form IT–201, 92–94, 98
New York State Form IT–201–ATT, 93, 96–97
New York State Form MV–44, 98–101
New York State Form MV–82, 99, 102, 103
New York State Form MV–500, 104–5

Open-ended format, 17
Operational criteria, 8
Operational design requirements, 28

Paper, 35
Paperwork excesses, 106
Paperwork Reduction Act of 1980, 69
Passive voice, 119
Perceptual breakdown, 36
Perceptual group, 35
Performance measure, 8
Personal-survey data form, 125–26
Phrasing, 52–53
Picas, 36
Pictorial symbols, 31. *See also* Coding
Pictures, use of, 32
Pie charts, 160
Pilot-interview form, 145, 147
Pilot studies, 26
Planning, 3

Political pressures for form changes, 69, 90, 106
Preferred-borrowers-screening form, 115–16
Prefixes, 23
Pretest, 31
Print: color, 32; contrast, 32, 33, 59; costs, 6, 30; dimension, 33; size, 33; stroke, 32, 33; style, 32
Prior processing, 40
Private sector, 65, 67–68
Procurement, 5, 7, 8
Product design questionnaires, 144–49
Product engineering, 140
Product-improvement forms, 139, 140
Productivity, 106
Product scheduling, 14
Products-available-to-stockholders form, 111, 113
Programming artifacts, 8
Programming the computer, 153–54
Promotion-and-intake forms, 109–27
Publisher-survey data form, 123–24

Quality control, 16
Quantitative requirements, 144
Questionnaire, administering, 147
Questionnaire sample items, 13, 163–67; least-to-most, 163; ranking, 164; selection of preferred area, 165; semantic differential, 166

Rational analysis, 10
Rational assessment, 61–62
Rationale, 10, 11
Readability 5, 29, 32, 33, 35, 44, 45, 104, 142
Readability formula, 62
Reading angle, 40
Reading comprehension, 48–49; development of, 51–61
Reading level, 48–49, 50, 61; elementary school, 51–52; preschool, 51, 52
Reading skill, 62
Recall, 38
Recognition, 28
Redundancy, 142
Repair-technician respondents, 147
Replication, 147
Representative sample, 140, 147
Resource management, 136
Respondent data, 141; inadequacies in, 143–44
Respondent population, 4, 7, 21, 25, 48–49, 50, 59, 62, 90, 143, 144, 145, 147
Respondents, 7, 24, 26, 38, 44 45, 47, 50, 52, 56, 61, 62, 63, 92, 112, 115, 127, 141, 152, 154
Response lags, 127, 130
Response time, 130
Rewriting for clarity, 54–55

Safety analysis forms, 139
Sales relations, 13
Same-side reference material, 125
Sampling, 25
Sectionalizing, 36
Sentence length, 22
Sequencing, 104
Service and repair, 145

Signage, 29
Silhouettes, 31, 81
Simplification, 10, 50
Situation response, 128
Slang, 51–52
Small-claims court claims form, 61
Soliciting-borrowers form, 117–18
Source documents, 154
Standard business-reply forms, 128–30, 131
State income-tax forms, 92–98
State of Michigan drivers' manual, 61
Storage, 5, 7
Stroke-to-height ratio, 33, 34. *See also* Printing
Subordinate clause, 53
Supplemental forms-derived management data, 157
Symbols. *See* Signage
Syntax and grammar, 47
System generalists, 152
Systems analysis, 3
Systems approach, 1–8; functions allocation in, 3; objectives of, 3

Tabular format, 56–59
Task simplification, 38–39
Technical terms, 24, 52, 87, 98, 121, 144
Temporal sequencing, 36
Terseness, 21, 22, 26
Testing, 25
Textbook-review form, 111, 112
Timeliness, 8
Transmission, 7
Type. *See* Print

Upper- and lower-case print, 76, 121, 123
User responses, 143
U.S. Postal Service Form 3573, 91–92; color coding, 92; fill-in, 92
U.S. Postal Service Form 3575, 90–92; color coding in, 92; content of, 90; fill-in, 92; print in, 92

Verbal content, 21–26, 27
Visual acuity, 33, 35
Visual angle, 33
Visual scanning, 28

Word arrangement, 36
Word-difficulty measure, 62
Words, using familiar, 23
Words classified by source, 51
Word-usage standards, 51
W-2 form, 71, 80